796·51

SRUC

TERRY MARSH

ON FOOT IN THE LAKE DISTRICT

SOUTHERN
& EASTERN FELLS

David & Charles

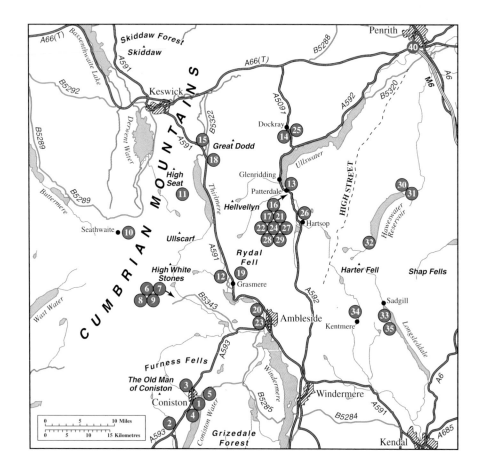

All photographs and maps are by the author

This book has been compiled in accordance with the *Guidelines for the Writers of Path Guides* produced by the Outdoor Writers' Guild. Every effort has been made to ensure that the information it contains about pathways is accurate, but changes do occur, and the author would welcome notification of any such changes, through the publisher.

A DAVID & CHARLES BOOK

First published 1997
Reprinted 2002

ISBN 0 7153 0368 6

Typeset by ABM Typographics Ltd, Hull
Printed in Italy by Milanostampa SpA
for David & Charles
Brunel House Newton Abbot Devon

Front cover photo: The central and eastern fells from above Tilberthwaite
Rear cover photo: The Coniston Fells from the Old Man of Coniston

CONTENTS

INTRODUCTION

The eastern side of the Lake District is very much the region's shop window. You pass by on the M6 motorway, for example, and glance across. What do you see? – the shapely cone of Kidsty Pike and the hump-back whale of High Street. Or, as you approach from the south, the great mound of Black Combe leads the eye to more attractive shapes, the Coniston fells, Crinkle Crags, Bow Fell and the unmistakable Langdale Pikes. Come to northern England from southern Scotland and it is the dark forms of Skiddaw, Blencathra and the rounded Dodds that draw the attention.

And while these are the eye-catching displays found in any shop window, around them lies a cornucopia of delight and more than enough 'trinkets' and 'bargains' to last a lifetime. Certainly there is far more than the most masterly vocabulary can embrace. As you tramp among the dales and ridges and describe the scenes, the rivers and lakes, the woodlands, the bird-song, the ever-changing light, and take on board the history and culture of the place, you soon exhaust all the superlatives, all the clichés, all the hackneyed expressions, assuming we wanted to use them in the first place.

Some of the best and gifted writing about Lakeland during the 1960s and 1970s came from the pen of Harry Griffin. He produced many books about the Lakeland he loved and which inspired him. His words, even on the tenth re-reading, guide you along as you search for the 'inner persona' of Lakeland I mention in the introduction to the final section in this book. The quest is, however, best summarised in the Foreword to Griffin's *In the Real Lakeland*, in which Lord Birkett relates how the author describes 'the authentic Lakeland, seen through the eyes of one who lives there all through the changing year, and who sees it in all seasons and all moods, and he writes with a kind of inward glow that comes from inside knowledge gained through years of experience'. It is that inward glow that we all seek; the means to its achievement is plainly stated – 'years of experience'. You cannot, as many modern tourists claim, 'do' the Lake District in a matter of days. There is simply too much to see and, what is worse, you see only those things that occur while you are there. To begin to scratch the surface you need permanency of residence, or, if that cannot be achieved, a constant to-ing and fro-ing over a long period of time. Only then will you begin to put flesh on the bones of your knowledge.

Although I do not live in the Lake District, within seconds I can be in a country park near my home with the dogs, and can peer through a gap in the trees, beyond the heathery fells of the Forest of Bowland, to the far blue hills of the Lakes. Within an hour I can be there, adding to the knowledge I have acquired over more than thirty years. At times I was in the Lakes every week, rampaging about, doing my wardenly duty; at other times exploring corners I never knew existed. And yet, even now, as I discovered while working on this book, there remain places and pathways I have never visited. If any region as small and compact as the Lake District can keep its secrets from an inquiring and working mind over so many years, it must be truly remarkable. And so it is.

In this volume on the southern and eastern fells, I explore the ever-popular ranges of Helvellyn and Fairfield, the Langdale summits, the Coniston fells, and the wild regions around High Street. But I also visit less well-known areas north of the Langdales, east of High Street and among the secret folds of the high fells. Not all walks are high-level, and I

The Central Fells of Lakeland from Helvellyn

have elected to include a walk or two around lakeshores, pursuing a fascination many visitors have for waterside walks.

It is a pious hope that attempts to convey to walkers the true essence of one of Britain's most endearing regions in a mere seventy walks – it would take many volumes, as Wainwright demonstrated. Some of the deficiency is rectified, I hope, by the pictures I have taken to illustrate the book, but since you can take precisely the same picture on each day of the year and produce three hundred and sixty five different images, even that becomes a forlorn hope. All I can wish for is that you will take some of my enthusiasm and love for the Lake District, add to it a dimension and purpose of your own, and then go in search of your own Lakeland destiny. One of the surest ways I know of getting there in the end, is to imagine you are writing a book and impose on yourself the regime and discipline that requires; don't charge about all over the place like a headless chicken: get to know select areas in detail before moving on. At the end of many years, preferably On Foot in the Lake District, you will be close to that exquisite satisfaction that only such an intimate and dedicated relationship with the Lakes can bring.

Grisedale Tarn

EXPLANATORY NOTES

The Walks

With over five hundred fell tops in the Lake District, it follows that there are an enormous number of ways of reaching their summits, and of devising routes between them. The thirty-five walks contained in this volume can do no more than hint at the emormous range of possibilities, but it is a hint with a distinctive flavour, one intended to encourage the interested reader to begin an exploration of this remarkable and popular region.

All the walks are circular and almost all follow clear paths, but where this is not so a note to that effect is given in the text, usually advising that the walk is not to be attempted in poor visibility.

None of the walks presents technical difficulties in good conditions in summer. Most are walks not climbs, though a few – Striding Edge and Swirral Edge, for example – need the ability to scramble. The majority of the walks can also be completed in good winter conditions, but when snow and ice prevail an ice axe is essential and crampons may be needed from time to time.

I have assumed that readers are sufficiently skilled in map and compass technique to pursue the text on the appropriate map and on the ground. Equally, it is taken that walkers will know how to clothe and protect themselves effectively against all weathers, and that they understand the uses of an ice axe and crampons where necessary.

Maps

The maps that accompany the walks are purely for a general indication of the route. They are, of course, no substitute for conventional maps, such as those described below.

The Ordnance Survey® Outdoor Leisure maps, to a scale of 1:25 000 (2½in to 1 mile – 4cm to 1km), cover all the walks and provide excellent detail. To complete all of the walks presented in this book you will need Sheets 4 (The English Lakes North Western area), 5 (The English Lakes North Eastern area), 6 (The English Lakes South Western area) and 7 (The English Lakes South Eastern area).

The Ordnance Survey Landranger Series Sheets 89 (West Cumbria), 90 (Penrith, Keswick and Ambleside) and 96 (Barrow-in-Furness and South Lakeland area), at a scale of 1:50 000 (1¼in to 1 mile – 2cm to 1km), cover the walks fully.

Harveys produce two maps – Southern Lakeland and Eastern Lakeland – which cover most of the area dealt with in this volume, except for the walks in Mardale, Kentmere and Longsleddale. These maps, intended specifically for walkers, are in two forms: one, the conventional Walker's series, at a scale of 1:40 000 (2.5cm to 1km), the other, the Superwalker series, to a scale of 1:25 000. Both series are produced on waterproof material, show different land usage and are accompanied by visitor guides.

Distances

The stated distances are for the *complete* walk. They are given in both metric and imperial measurements and have been rounded up or down.

Height Gain

This reflects the total ascent for the walk as described, not just the height gain from the start to the top of a fell.

Walking Times

These represent a realistic allowance for a walker of average fitness but it must be stressed **they make no allowance for stops**, other than brief halts to take pictures.

Sections and Section Names

These are arbitrary, should not be taken too seriously and are simply creatures of convenience.

Access

It is unlikely you will be challenged on any of these walks if you stick to the routes described. But the Lake District is a working environment, one that needs to be treated sensitively by visitors. Any mention of a path **does not imply that a right of way exists**. If you are asked not to follow a particular route, please comply, as there is invariably a good reason for doing so.

If you take your dog with you, please ensure it is held on a leash at all times. Do not allow your dog to run about unrestrained.

CONISTON

Among today's visitors, the fells of Coniston are as popular as any in the Lake District and they and the surrounding area are visited, sooner or later, by everyone who ventures into this remarkable corner of pre-1974 Lancashire. Coniston's modern history is one of tourism built on the legacy of a mining, sheep farming and quarrying past, that itself evolved over thousands of years from primeval chaos.

Following the retreat of the glaciers that left behind a landscape of turmoil, everywhere became colonised by trees, remote from the eye of the inquisitive and home only to early man, who lived on the high moors of Torver, Blawith and Monk Coniston. For these early settlers the main interest lay in the extensive woodlands, a great, if limited, DIY storehouse from which to build their homes and construct weapons and tools.

In the early twelfth century much of the area, then known as Furness, was given to a colony of monks from the Norman-French abbey at Savigny. They founded an abbey at Furness, and in 1143 resisted the parent abbey's move to the Cistercian Order, for which the abbot, Peter of York, was captured and held in France. He became a most worthy monk, learning the Cistercian Order. His abbey meanwhile was run by a Frenchman, by whose diligence and counsel the abbey at Furness succumbed to the new Order. It was the influence of the abbey that shaped much of the landscape we see today around Coniston, for they cleared most of the forest to make charcoal to fire the bloomeries for the copper mines and to develop grazing for sheep.

For five hundred years the area around Coniston was scoured for copper, a source both of considerable prosperity and of dereliction, and the relics of these mines provide endless fascination for industrial archaeologists. Now, Coniston no longer relies on such robber industries for its economy but on tourism and boating.

Yet it was only with the opening of the Furness Railway in 1859, originally intended for more efficient transportation of copper and slate, that tourism began to flourish. By the time author and art critic John Ruskin came to live on the shores of Coniston Water, tourism was well established; Keswick and Ambleside had a host of new and old hotels, while a complete new town of boarding houses and shops had developed at Windermere.

But it is with the fells around Coniston that we are concerned, a mosaic of lofty mountains and fine valleys, in spite of the ravages of industry. Few in number, the Coniston fells form a compact assortment of features that stand among the most endearing in the Lake District. They are composed of the rugged rocks of the Borrowdale Volcanic Series but lie at the southernmost extremity of high mountain Lakeland, abruptly yielding to the softer folds of Silurian moorland.

Most of the fells embrace what is known as the Coppermines Valley, with only a few outliers – Grey Friar and the Dow Crag ridge – guarding the western flank and overlooking the secret glades and pastures of the Duddon valley. To the north, the Coniston fells are restrained by the line of the Wrynose Pass, at the head of which the Three Shire Stone marks the boundaries of the former counties of Lancashire, Westmorland and Cumberland.

To the east the woodlands around Tarn Hows, surely one of Lakeland's best-loved sanctuaries, form a delightful 'book-end' before the southern fells are left for the vastly contrasting landscapes of the central and eastern fells. Here, in this man-made setting, I offer a walk that characterises all that is good about Lakeland walking, one that, for a change, disposes of the need for long and arduous ascents, replacing them with self-indulgent meandering. To range from these extremes is, for the fells of Coniston, an easy task, for in the Coniston portfolio there is something for everyone.

Wetherlam

THE OLD MAN OF CONISTON

I would hazard a guess that every Lakeland fell top is visited by someone during the course of a year. Some may receive only a few pairs of feet; others countless thousands. The Old Man of Coniston will almost certainly be in the top ten, for it has magnetic appeal and repays magnificently the effort of reaching its summit. This ascent begins along Church Beck before climbing through the old quarries to reach Low Water and the final haul to the summit.

From the main car park in Coniston, go left into the village and across the bridge, turning right along a minor road to the Sun Hotel. Here turn immediately right on a signposted path to the Old Man and Levers Water that pursues the course of Church Beck.

This pleasant start soon leads to a bridge at the entrance to Coppermines Valley (1). Keep left at this point, continuing on a less broad path, over stiles, and gaining height steadily as you rise to meet a well-constructed track at a bend. Turn right, following the track as it

Looking north from the Old Man of Coniston

twists upwards through increasingly rough terrain and the spoil of quarrying generations past. Only a keen industrial archaeologist would find the untidy scenes of turmoil and dereliction attractive, yet the many tumbled piles of slate, the rusted machinery and defunct buildings, arouse curiosity about the men who toiled here, the hardships they faced and the many dangers.

Some of the dangers are still present, especially if you venture near the main quarry, a vast hollow hacked from the hill but unseen from the main path. At the top of a rise the path bends left then right. If, before turning right, you continue ahead, you encounter a vast cavern, created by quarrymen. It is very dangerous now, having suffered roof collapses in the recent past. **Do not enter**, under any circumstances.

Return to the main path and ascend (now left) to reach Low Water **(2)** reposing in an enormous cirque of cliffs and steep, unstable slopes. This is one of Lakeland's grandest settings, the hue of the water, tinted blue by copper, injecting brightness into the scene.

The top of the Old Man lies directly above but to reach it you must follow a rough and steep path zigzagging across the south wall of this corrie. Once at the top, turn right, and follow a broad, shaly path to the summit. The

Low Water and the final section up to the Old Man of Coniston

Start/Finish Main car park in Coniston,
GR 303976
Distance 7.5km (4³/₄ miles)
Height gain 750m (2460ft)
Walking time 4 hours
Type of walk A rocky trail, on clear paths. Parts
can be confusing in mist and the summit trig is
very close to a steep drop

The Route in Brief
Start Leave Coniston past the Sun Hotel and go
R on a path leading into the Coppermines Valley.
1 Follow a rising path across the south side of
the valley to reach broad track. Climb up through
old quarry workings to reach Low Water.
2 Ascend zigzagging path out of corrie and at
top, bear R, to follow broad path to summit.

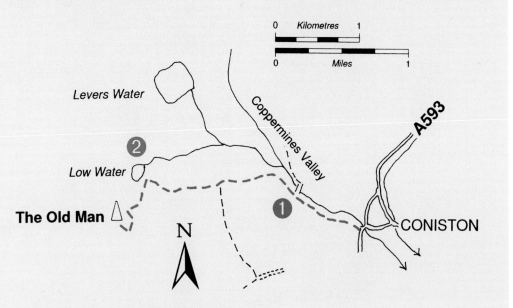

trig pillar is in a commanding position overlooking the Low Water basin.

The Old Man of Coniston was first ascended in 1792 by Captain Joseph Budworth, who
had already that day walked from Ambleside
to Coniston to see the lake and found himself
unable to resist the challenge of the fell.
Sustained only by brandy, he completed the
first ascent and still walked back to Ambleside!

The top of the mountain used to possess
three stone beacons – 'the Old Man', his
'Wife' and 'Son'. The largest of the three had
a small chamber that provided rudimentary
shelter. The disappearance of the beacons, it is
alleged, was occasioned by Ordnance Survey
engineers.

The measured distances and height gain for
this walk assume a return by the outward
route; a sufficient and satisfying prospect,
without needing to extend the day any further.
Those with time, energy and inclination to do
so can effect a more circuitous return by continuing briefly northwards from the Old Man
before descending, left, on a rough path, to
reach Goat's Hause, north-east of Goat's
Water. From this broad, boggy col you can
either descend to Goat's Water and follow a
good path out to the Walna Scar Road, or
ascend Dow Crag, to follow the long, undulating ridge to the Walna Scar Pass, as
described in Walk 2.

DOW CRAG AND GOAT'S WATER

Offering both a challenge and dramatic mountain scenery, this traverse of the Dow Crag-Brown Pike ridge, the watershed between the Coniston valley and Dunnerdale, begins from Torver. It starts by visiting old quarries before rising to the ancient, and almost certainly prehistoric, trail route, Walna Scar road, which once echoed to the sound of pack-horses carrying slate. Much of the land crossed forms part of Torver High Common, a rocky and remarkable terrain of rolling bracken and heather that, as William Collingwood, sometime private secretary to John Ruskin, observed, 'must once have been the happy hunting-grounds of primitive races, children of the mist'.

The walk sets off from a lay-by on the A593, just north of Torver, by a surfaced lane signposted to Coniston Old Man and Walna Scar. Judicious waymarking steers you through Scar Head village to reach a walled bridleway. At the third gate spanning the track, go through a gate and cross Tranearth Beck, continuing on a rough track to a group of sheep pens.

More waymarking (in blue) takes you to a

On the Walna Scar Road

Goat's Water

wooden bridge over Torver Beck, beyond which you turn left to pass between quarry spoil heaps and climb beside a tree-lined gully. The gully is the entrance to the Bannishead Quarry and is dangerous. Ascend to a fence and go right, circling the quarry and follow a terraced path on the left, rising to meet Walna Scar road **(1)**.

As you walk, left, along Walna Scar road and cross Torver Beck once more, you become conscious of a clear distinction between the land forms to the north and those to the south. Walna Scar road roughly corresponds with the interface between the softer Silurian strata to the south, with its gentler, rolling form, and the more rugged rocks of the Borrowdale Volcanic Series to the north. Between the two runs a sliver of quite different rocks – Stockdale Shales and Coniston Limestone. The resultant interplay provides the most fascinating scenery.

Gradually, the Walna Scar road becomes more broken and negotiates occasional rock outcrops before finally reaching a small cairn at the top of the pass **(2)**. A breathtaking view across Dunnerdale awaits. If you have time (less than an hour should suffice) and energy to spare, you could go left here across the grassy mound called Walna Scar and out to White Maiden and White Pike, beyond which stand the rough bounds of the Dunnerdale Fells.

If you decide not to extend the walk then turn right from the pass and ascend easily to

Brown Pike, the mid-point of a long, descending ridge, of which White Maiden and White Pike are the southerly part.

The way now lies northwards, scarcely moving away from the rising edge overlooking Goat's Water and following a clear path, first over Buck Pike, before finally reaching the craggy top of Dow Crag (3). Only in the vicinity of Goat's Water will you truly appreciate the magnificence of the cliffs, described by Harriet Martineau as '…crags piled in grotesque fashion…' These lie below Dow Crag's summit but this lofty, isolated perch compensates by providing extensive seaward views, across Dunnerdale, Ulpha Fell and Muncaster to the coast at Ravenglass, and northwards to the high central fells of Lakeland.

Dow Crag, generally accepted as rhyming with 'hoe' rather than 'how', eases northwards, curving east as it descends to Goat's Hawse, from where tracks radiate north, south, east and west. East rises the Old Man of Coniston, a tiring, toilsome trek; north the fellside falls gently to the hidden valley housing Seathwaite Tarn, beneath the great flanks of Grey Friar.

The walk continues south, descending from the hause to the very edge of Goat's Water (4); care is needed on the descent. Now, the cliffs of Dow Crag take on their true perspective, rising magnificently from above the tarn in a defiant challenge that few Lakeland rock climbers are able to resist.

When mist fills this mountain hollow, the atmosphere is eerie and imbued with a sense of foreboding: in the brightness of a spring day you revel in the power of beautiful enthusiasms, for life, for living, for the landscape, for the very rocks that support the stage of Lakeland drama.

A good path leads away from Goat's Water to a large cairn on the Walna Scar road, not far from the point at which you first joined it. Cross the 'road' to a green path and descend to the fence above Bannishead Quarry, from where you can easily retrace your steps to Torver.

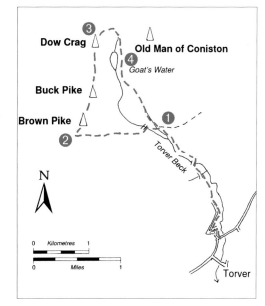

FACT FILE

Start/Finish Lay-by on A593 near Torver, GR 285945
Distance 11km (6³/₄ miles)
Height gain 670m (2198ft)
Walking time 5–6 hours
Type of walk A demanding high fell walk, on good paths

The Route in Brief
Start Leave the A593 and follow track through Scar Head, past Bannishead Quarry and up to join the Walna Scar road.
1 Go L and ascend to Walna Scar Pass.
2 Ascend N on to Brown Pike and Buck Pike, to reach Dow Crag.
3 Descend to Goat's Hawse and from there to Goat's Water.
4 Follow clear path out of valley to rejoin Walna Scar road. Keep ahead on green path, down to Bannishead Quarry and retrace steps.

TILBERTHWAITE GILL AND WETHERLAM

A popular tourist place during Victorian times, Tilberthwaite Gill is a natural gorge of considerable beauty, through which flows Yewdale Beck, though the stream is generally known as Tilberthwaite Gill. Such was its fame that the Victorians developed precarious footpaths linking flimsy wooden bridges to view the spectacle.

The region also saw its share of slate quarrying during the nineteenth century, though the evidence of it today is considerably less unsightly than it is among the Coniston fells that lie to the south-west.

Overlording the gill, and a landscape that has notable appeal, rises Wetherlam, a fine, rugged, satisfying summit, here ascended from Tilberthwaite by a justifiably popular route.

The hamlet of Low Tilberthwaite lies secreted within enfolding fells along a minor road that runs acutely away from the A593 about 2.5km (1½ miles) north of Coniston. Take care as you drive along this winding road – the scenery is a great distraction.

From the lower edge of a commodious (but in summer inadequate) car park a flight of slate steps ascends quickly through quarry spoil to a path junction. On the way you pass Penny Rigg Quarry, which is worth a peek, but keep children and dogs under control since there are sudden and unfenced drops within the quarry.

At the path junction you have a choice of ways. Either go right, and descend to a bridge spanning Tilberthwaite Gill continuing steeply (on an unstable footpath) to a stile, across which you join a former miners' track, then turning left. Or climb left for a little pleasant cavorting with rocky knuckles (slippery when wet), before the path opens out and swings round to head towards Crook Beck (1).

More evidence of quarrying now appears in a vast mountain arena that is a fascinating place for the curious; but a dangerous one, too. Slate quarrying has been a lasting source of wealth for the Lakeland economy, though inland quarries, like those above Tilberthwaite, had a limited period of prosperity, often supplying only a local market. Yet, as long ago as 1818, merchants, like Thomas Rigge of Hawkshead, were exporting Tilberthwaite green slate, carrying it via Coniston Water to Greenodd, from where it went by sloop to seaports throughout England and Ireland.

Pass through the quarrying area, but *do* keep well away from shafts and adits. By a footbridge, cross Tilberthwaite Gill and climb to the miners' track joined earlier by walkers who chose to cross the gill lower down. Turn left along the track to begin a splendid, rising walk that visits the ruins of Hellen's Mine and skirts the marshlands of Dry Cove, once flooded to provide power for a water wheel at the Tilberthwaite Mine. You then arrive at the Borlase Mine, high above the cove.

Take a rough but enjoyable path, ascending right in zigzags to reach Birk Fell Hawse (2), a narrow neck of land linking Wetherlam and nearby Birk Fell. This upper section of the walk, with its retrospective view of Dry Cove and the quarrylands beyond, is splendid; the arrival at Birk Fell Hawse, even better. For here, the ground falls almost unnoticed across Greenburn, before sprawling onwards across the fells above Langdale and out to the distant Scafells.

The ascent to the top of Wetherlam now pursues a fine, rocky (and, if you want it, scrambly) ridge, networked by paths, all of which guide you ever upwards. The top of the fell (3) is a vast rocky platform with views as

Wetherlam from the top of Tilberthwaite Gill

FACT FILE

Start/Finish Tilberthwaite car park, GR 306010
Distance 8km (5 miles)
Height gain 570m (1870ft)
Walking time 4–5 hours
Type of walk A fine, high fell outing that is rough in places. Good, former miners' tracks used throughout the lower sections, though the top of Wetherlam is confusing in mist

The Route in Brief

Start Leave the car park by a flight of steps up to a path leading towards Tilberthwaite Gill. At a fork, climb L on a rocky path that leads round to meet Crook Beck, or go R and descend to cross the gill, climbing steeply to a miners' track, and then L until just above the confluence of Tilberthwaite Gill and Crook Beck.

1 Follow continuing miners' track, swinging high above Dry Cove and climbing steadily to Birk Fell Hawse, above Greenburndale.

2 Climb, L (SW) to the top of Wetherlam.

3 Set off S towards a large cairn, and then by long descending path to reach top of Hole Rake Pass.

4 Go L (NE), past small tarn, and return to Crook Beck. Retrace outward route from there, or recross bridge used earlier and turn R to descend to Low Tilberthwaite, and car park.

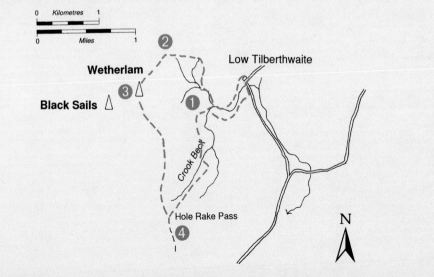

far-reaching as Ingleborough in Craven. Much nearer lies the Old Man of Coniston and Swirl How, separated by the modest hump of Brim Fell. Among the summit rocks there are many nooks in which to shelter or you could press on towards a conspicuous cairn to the south (signalling the eventual way off), and then deviate to the right for a secluded break gazing across at the Old Man.

The cairn lies along a gradually improving path that descends for quite some distance through rocky knolls and tarn-filled hollows – a delightful experience – eventually moving left (south-east) to fall gradually to a path near the top of Hole Rake Pass (**4**). Go left, along the path, passing a small reed-filled tarn and continue north-east and north, in the company of Crook Beck, until you ultimately return to the quarry site at the head of Tilberthwaite Gill.

You can return to the car park quickly by turning right along the path on the south side of the gill, or, preferably, recross the footbridge ahead (used earlier), and turn right to reach the miners' track. Go right again, now descending the track, with Tilberthwaite Gill below on the right, and continue a pleasurable descent to a gate/wall just above Low Tilberthwaite.

Continue with the path, down and round to the small group of cottages below, where you will find a fine example of a cottage with a spinning gallery, from which wool would once have been hung to dry. On reaching the road, the car park is only a few short strides away to the right.

THE CONISTON ROUND

The Coniston Fells are obliged to suffer the ravages of man's industrial endeavours rather more than any other group of fells in the Lake District. Yet the charisma of this fine collection of summits is such that they succeed with very little effort in rising proudly above the chaos that scars their flanks and probes deeply beneath them in search of hidden wealth. In this grand tour, you take in five outstanding summits, literally in one fell swoop, promenading high above the Coppermines Valley, with fine panoramas to draw the eye away from the dereliction below.

Begin from the centre of Coniston, leaving across the bridge and up past the Sun Hotel, there turning right on a path signposted to the Old Man. This is the route taken by Walk 1 and it rises with Church Beck to enter the Coppermines Valley, crosses named pastures – Foul Scrow and Levers Moss Scrow – and rises to meet a broad miners' track at Crowberry Haws.

Follow the track as it rambles through quarry spoil to reach Low Water, before scampering up the southern wall of the corrie in

Swirl How and Black Sails from Wetherlam

19

Start/Finish Coniston car park, GR 303976
Distance 12km (7¹/₂ miles)
Height gain 1075m (3525ft)
Walking time 5–6 hours
Type of walk Following well-established paths, this high mountain route is generally straightforward, but the descent of Prison Band in winter conditions could prove awkward

The Route in Brief

Start Follow Walk 1 to the summit of the Old Man of Coniston.
1 Continue N over Brim Fell and Levers Hawse to reach Swirl How.
2 Descend N of E, down Prison Band and on across Black Sails, before rising to Wetherlam.
3 Set off S to a large cairn and then follow long descending path to top of Hole Rake Pass.
4 Continue down into Coppermines Valley, going L to Miners' Bridge, and cross bridge to meet outward route.

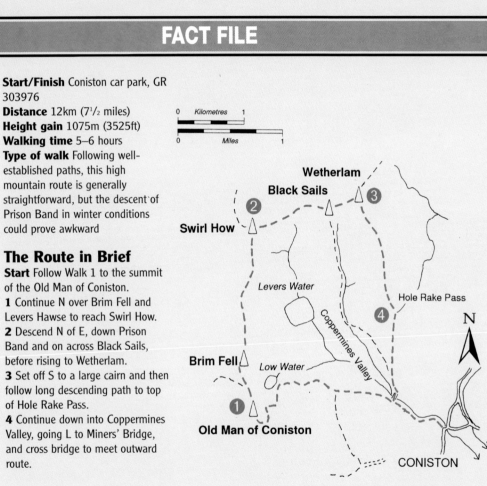

which the tarn lies, to reach a broad and rough track up to the summit of the Old Man (1).

Keeping parallel with the rim of the corrie, go north across Brim Fell, a wide grassy, rock-studded fell, and descend to Levers Hawse. This col directly overlooks Levers Water, to which an escape can be made if necessary.

A brief pull takes you on over Little and Great How Crags before striding on to the small rocky plateau of Swirl How (2), which has the best of both worlds, overlooking both the upper reaches of Coppermines Valley and the wide hollow of Greenburndale.

From Swirl How a steep, rocky and loose rib, Prison Band, descends north of east to the narrow gap of Swirl Hawse, beyond which easy walking leads up on to Black Sails. A short descent to Red Dell Head Moss preludes one final, rocky ascent to the top of Wetherlam (3), which proves to be an outstanding vantage point.

Just south of the summit of Wetherlam you can pick out a large cairn. Head for this and then trek down the ensuing and pleasant path above Hen Crag and the appropriately named Above Beck Fells – the beck being Crook Beck – in due course reaching the top of Hole Rake Pass (4). Turn right and follow the path down to Church Beck and the Coppermines Valley. Not long after reaching the lowest miners' track, you come to Miners' Bridge. Cross this to rejoin your outward route and retrace your steps to Coniston.

TARN HOWS

Any stay in the Coniston area would be incomplete without a visit to Tarn Hows, for in spite of a man-made pedigree the tarn blends well with the surrounding fells and is an inspiring, romantic place, almost too pretty. Motorists can reach it by a narrow lane from Coniston; walkers have delightful wooded ways to pursue. Around the lake, a thoughtfully graded path is well suited to handicapped walkers, though visitors in wheelchairs will need a strong companion for safety on some of the steeper inclines. This agreeable walk, also suitable for children, follows well-marked pathways and is at its best in early spring.

Easy walking on the Tarn Hows circuit

Start from the Waterhead car park and go left around the head of Coniston Water to meet the B5285. Cross the road and turn right, through a gate to follow a fenced path alongside the road. The path rejoins the road at Boon Crag Cottage **(1)**, near the turning to Boon Crag Farm. The cottage and farm used to be part of the vast Monk Coniston

Estate, now in the ownership of the National Trust. The estate formerly belonged to James Garth Marshall, Member of Parliament for Leeds, who studied the metamorphic rocks of the surrounding area and contributed significantly to modern geological understanding.

Go past Boon Crag Cottage and the farm turning, and after the next cottage, go left through a gate into a field. Keeping parallel with the B-road, press on to reach the side road that leads up to Tarn Hows. Cross it to reach a bridleway (signposted to Tarn Hows) and follow this, rising gradually and pleasantly through pines, past a series of small pools and through a wall gap, until the track levels, before crossing a beck.

Keep on, ignoring branching pathways, until you arrive at a fork. Go right, ascending by a narrowing path beside a wall. Soon, turn left, once more on a wider trail, and follow a wall to meet a road, beyond which lies a parking area for the disabled. Within strides you are following a well-made track that completely circles Tarn Hows (2), a fascinating tour, with outstanding views and reassuring glimpses of familiar fells, among them the Old Man of Coniston, Wetherlam, the Langdale Pikes and perhaps Helvellyn on a clear day.

It is far from evident these days, but Tarn Hows was originally created to supply water to a saw mill in Yewdale, its overflow spilling

Tarn Hows

in dashing style down the ravine of Tom Gill. Later, it was owned by Mrs William Heelis, better known as Beatrix Potter, who sold half to the National Trust for what it cost to buy, and bequeathed the remainder.

Anyone wanting a much briefer visit to Tarn Hows can ascend through delightful oak woodlands from Glen Mary Bridge, via Tom Gill, visiting its shady, crag-enfolded waterfall. John Ruskin, who lived at Brantwood on the shores of Coniston Water, felt Tom Gill deserved a more picturesque name and so bestowed upon it the title 'Glen Mary', hence Glen Mary Bridge, at its foot.

The complete circuit of the tarn brings you back to the outflow, beyond which you go through a gate to a track ascending to the road. Follow the road, right, past the car park and continue for almost half a mile (about ¾km) to a signposted footpath on the right. The path, flanked by a wall and mature oak woodland, leads to Tarn Hows Cottage (3).

Take a path signposted to Low Yewdale and Coniston, passing through two gates before turning right on to a broad, descending track to Yewdale Beck. Go left, beside the beck, cross a stile, heading for a gate and bridge. Do not cross the beck.

Through a gate, turn left still beside the beck and then rising between walls and fences before easing down to Boon Crag Farm (4). Keep on, between farm buildings to rejoin the main road at Boon Crag Cottage, where you turn right, to retrace your steps to the car park.

FACT FILE

Start/Finish Waterhead car park, GR 316978
Distance 8km (5 miles)
Height gain 280m (920ft)
Walking time 2–3 hours
Type of walk Simple and delightful, on good paths throughout

The Route in Brief

Start Leave the car park and go L to a road junction. Cross to gate, and turn R along fenced path to Boon Crag Cottage.
1 Pass entrance to Boon Crag Farm, enter field and continue to meet lane ascending L to Tarn Hows. Cross on to bridleway and follow this to Tarn Hows.
2 Circle Tarn Hows, and return to outflow and gate. Rise to road and turn, R, down it to path leading to Tarn Hows Cottage.
3 Continue towards Low Yewdale Farm and on to Boon Crag Farm.
4 Between farm buildings to road. Turn right and retrace steps to car park.

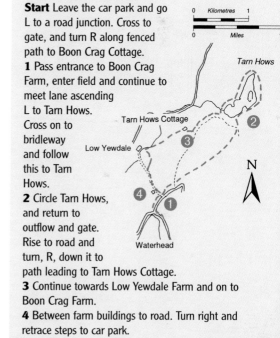

2

THE CENTRAL FELLS

The group of summits that gather under the umbrella of the Central Fells are brought together as much out of convenience as from any geographical exactitude. One of them, Ullscarf, is generally accepted as the most central fell in the Lake District and is part of a broad, elongated grassy ridge with an unhappy propensity for retaining water. As a result, these Wythburn Fells offer much scope for peaceful wandering.

Other self-contained groupings also belong to the Central Fells, those that circle Langdale and the Borrowdale Fells. Few in number, the latter comprise only those steep-sided fells along the eastern flank of Borrowdale's southernmost reaches. They are bounded on the west by the long arm that runs to Seathwaite and up Grains Gill to Esk Hause, and on the east by Langstrathdale. To go up one side and down the other is a fine outing in itself, and avoids mountain tops completely, though Allen Crags, Esk Pike and Rossett Pike are all within bagging distance.

The greatest attraction of this centre ground, however, lies in the massive wall of fells at the head of Langdale, where Crinkle Crags and Bow Fell maintain their ranking in the Lakeland 'Top Ten' of the most-visited summits. What visitors know as Langdale is really Great Lang-

dale, for this popular dale has a less dramatic but in its own way equally attractive, counterpart in Little Langdale, that branches from the main thrust near Elterwater and rises to the Wrynose Pass, and itself sub-divides to provide the rarely visited enclave of Greenburndale.

The main Langdale valley is unique among Lakeland valleys in not having the more conventional 'straight trough' formation but one that is twisting. At its western end the valley divides, one branch, Mickleden, aligned north-west–south-east, and the other, Oxendale, flows south-west–north-east. Both combine at Stool End at the eastern end of a great wedge of rising ground known as The Band.

Langdale has long been popular, indeed it is known to have been the site of a sizeable stone axe factory during prehistoric times, with a trade claimed to extend as far as Europe. Much of this interest centred on the slopes of Harrison Stickle and Pike of Stickle, along the northern flank, and the Langdale-Esk Hause-Sty Head-Aaron Slack-Ennerdale link must have been a convenient route to the coastal plains.

While not detracting from the unrivalled popularity of Crinkle Crags and Bow Fell, the group of summits collectively called the Langdale Pikes have a place in most fell walkers' hearts, though quite which 'pikes' com-

prise the 'Langdale Pikes' is both unclear and, in the scale of things, unimportant. This compact arrangement of fells provides splendid walking opportunity, one of Lakeland's finest rock scrambles, in Jack's Rake on Pavey Ark, and an outstanding array of rock climbs, particularly on the battlements that overlook the eastern end of Mickleden.

To the north-east of this area, the vast tract of ground known as Grasmere Common provides its own delights. Its main concentration focuses on Easedale and Far Easedale where just to walk the valleys is a pleasure in itself. Yet high ground surrounds the dales – bright-eyed tarns and white-water cataracts pierce the dark green or autumnal brown of bracken-clad fellsides and granite-grey outcrops punctuate the landscape.

On the very edge of this much-visited area the rocky top of Helm Crag has inspired imagination to call one grouping of rocks 'the Lion and the Lamb' and so unleashed an inordinate weight of interest and curiosity, that many weary legs will wish had never been aroused by the time the direct route to the summit is complete.

But it is characteristic of the Central Fells that they accommodate everyone, from the idly curious to the expert rock gymnast, from the fair-weather fell wanderer to the winter mountaineer in search of adventure.

Wetherlam and Great Langdale

CRINKLE CRAGS AND THREE TARNS

The crenallated profile of Crinkle Crags at the head of Great Langdale is at once both daunting and captivating, a splendid challenge for any walker who is at ease scampering about on rocky terrain. Quite often the ascent of Crinkle Crags is combined with its neighbour, Bow Fell, in what proves to be a superb outing for a summer's day, but this walk is restricted to a return via Three Tarns and The Band, so offering a walk for all seasons. The name, Crinkle Crags, derives not from its serrated outline, but from the Old Norse *kringla*, meaning a circle.

Start from the National Trust car park at Old Dungeon Ghyll and walk out along its access to meet the main valley road. Turn right for the short distance to the long access track to Stool End Farm. This approach, a considerable pleasure in early-morning sunlight, provides an enticing glimpse into Mickleden. Pike o'Stickle, Rossett Pike and Bow Fell form the main ring of summits,

Crinkle Crags and Oxendale

while Loft Crag's cliffs are a popular resort for rock climbers. Ahead, the wedge of The Band, the return route of this walk, forms a broad tongue between Bow Fell and Crinkle Crags.

On reaching Stool End Farm (1), follow the obvious way between the buildings, keeping left in the farmyard to a five-bar gate that gives access to the lower fell. A broad, stony track runs on beside a wall and soon forks. Keep ahead (left branch) to a gate, heading into Oxendale, and follow a wide track to and through a sheep enclosure. Oxendale Beck is crossed by a memorial bridge (2), beyond which a constructed path climbs mercilessly to the knoll of Brown Howe and a spectacular vision of Browney Gill. Throughout this ascent, the unavoidable toil is eased by ever-changing views of Bow Fell, above Hell Gill, and Crinkle Crags.

Once above Browney Gill, only brief bouts of uphill work remain before the path meets that arriving from Wrynose Pass, not far from (unseen) Red Tarn (3). Turn right on a rising path that brings Red Tarn into retrospective view, climbing steadily between the knobbly summit of Cold Fell (always worth a diversion) and Great Knott (likewise). The path presses on without undue effort to reach the first crinkle, South Top (4), by a short rocky

Crinkle Crags

scramble. Among its numerous wrinkles many cosy nooks provide shelter for a break.

A brief descent brings you to the only real problem of the whole outing, the Bad Step. From the col between South Top and the main summit, a conspicuous gully can be seen to be obstructed by two large blocks. If scrambling is not your *forte*, go left at the base of this gully on a slightly descending path that soon loops right and climbs easily to the summit.

Otherwise address the Bad Step. People of very small stature, or those who normally spend their leisure time in the subterranean

FACT FILE

Start/Finish Old Dungeon Ghyll Car Park (Pay and Display), GR 285061
Distance 11km (6¾ miles)
Height gain 840m (2755ft)
Walking time 5 hours
Type of walk Energetic start, followed by excellent rocky ridge walking with outstanding views. Modest scrambling on the Bad Step (avoidable)

The Route in Brief

Start Leave the car park, and walk out to the main valley road, turning R to T-junction and there ahead on long approach to Stool End Farm.
1 Go through farmyard, and L through gate to stony track. Keep ahead (L) at fork, to gate, and then track to sheep enclosure and bridge over valley stream.
2 Ascend steep, constructed path beyond, and continue to meeting of paths near Red Tarn.
3 Turn R and follow clear trail to the first crinkle, South Top.
4 Keep to clear (and cairned) path over all the crinkles and Shelter Crags to reach Three Tarns.
5 Turn R and descend The Band to Stool End. Retrace steps.

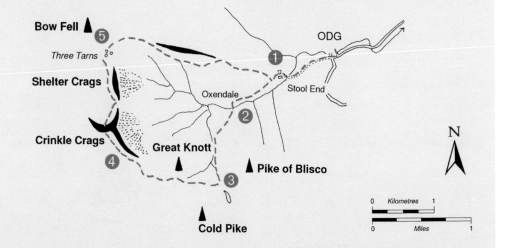

passages of the countryside, may find a way beneath the obstructing boulders, but it is very tight and claustrophobic for others.

The right wall of the gully provides the escape. There are three places where the rocks are now polished, indicating the routes taken by walkers; the lowest of these, a neat little corner, is for most the easiest and involves only a few brief moments of rock work before the upper path is gained and pursued to the summit, Long Top. The Bad Step can be awkward in winter conditions when the alternative route is advised.

The way on now lies over, but mostly around, the next three crinkles, with breathtaking views down scree gullies and cliff faces into Oxendale from each of them, or westwards, across the expanse of the Great Moss to Scafell and Scafell Pike. This section is quite delightful, with constantly changing cameos of the surrounding landscape.

One final crinkle, bearing the distinction of its own name, Shelter Crags, lies a distance apart, overlooking The Band and Hell Gill. Once beyond this, the path eases down to a broad, grassy col housing a collection of shallow puddles, the Three Tarns **(5)**, beneath the crags of Bow Fell Links.

A large cairn, on the right, marks the start of The Band, which proves to be rather longer than might be expected, but leads you on a clear path unerringly back to Stool End, from where your outward steps can be retraced.

BOW FELL AND ESK PIKE

Being the highest, the largest, the biggest, the most prominent, is always a guarantee of attention, and Bow Fell meets most, if not all, of those criteria. Anyone passing Lakeland by on the M6 motorway can look across and spot the unmistakable skyline of Langdale – rippling Crinkle Crags on the left and peaked Bow Fell on the right. Bow Fell is a wild and rocky mountain, its rock-strewn summit plateau as untidy as a child's playroom, its appeal unchallenged and a magnet for all: Bow Fell is in the Premier Division, and rightly so. Linked here with Esk Pike to make a grand rocky circuit fit for a fine summer's day; with suitable equipment and experience it makes an outstanding winter walk, too.

Leave the car park at the Old Dungeon Ghyll Hotel by its access lane, to the main valley road and turn right at a T-junction. Go ahead, through a gate and down the long access track to Stool End Farm **(1)**. Ahead, Crinkle Crags and Bow Fell extend

Bowfell from Crinkle Crags

Bowfell from the Band

it affords are excellent and ample reward for effort.

Before long you encounter the intake wall and gate, from where there is a superb view of the Langdale Pikes and the great scree run of Pike of Stickle. The path up The Band tends to favour the Oxendale side and for a long time the full form of Bow Fell is obscured. Gradually it toils onward, to finish with one last rocky flourish at the broad, damp col housing the Three Tarns (2). Directly ahead you are treated to a fine view of the Scafells.

The continuing way up Bow Fell is by a conspicuous scree slope, tiring, but not over-long, finishing with a final rocky crossing to the summit. So popular is Bow Fell (3) that it is unlikely you will ever have the summit to yourself; if you do find yourself alone, make the most of it; there is already someone grunting up the slopes from the Three Tarns!

Once determined to press on, the way to Esk Pike lies initially north, across a rock-studded terrain that can be confusing in misty conditions. Gradually the well-cairned path slips a degree or two west of north, before swinging west to descend to Ore Gap. From this obvious col you can descend, right, directly to Angle Tarn, if circumstances dictate. Otherwise, tackle the short pull on to Esk Pike (4), another rocky proposition, but without difficulty. The summit cairn on Esk Pike is perched on top of a large rocky outcrop.

invitations, both of which, on a long summer day, can be accepted in one combined outing.

Go through the farmyard and bear left to a gate, beyond which a gravelly path runs on beside a wall. When a path branches right a short way on, go with it to begin the long ascent of The Band, an elongated tongue of upland rising to the col between Bow Fell and Crinkle Crags, and separating the two branches of the Langdale valley, Mickleden and Oxendale. The ascent seems very long and can be tiring on a hot day but the views

Continue across the top of the mountain, to begin a gradual and rocky descent to Esk Hause shelter **(5)**, which lies just above a mountain path crossroads. Turn right at the shelter and descend to Angle Tarn, a splendid hollow, well-suited to a break. Beyond, the path pushes on to the steep-sided ravine of Rossett Gill **(6)**.

Rossett Gill has quite a reputation for hard labour, more so when used as an ascent. In descent, the effort is noticeably less, path improvement work having made the downward lunge considerably less fraught with dif-ficulty than it once was. An old packhorse route, zigzagging down the steep slopes, though a little longer, takes some of the sting out of the knees.

Once clear of the steepest ground, you can enjoy a pleasant descent to meet Stake Gill, beyond which the easiest of walking leads down through Mickleden, beneath the gaze of Pike of Stickle and Loft Crag, before becoming corralled by walls on the approach to the Old Dungeon Ghyll. The car park lies beyond one final gate at the rear of the hotel.

FACT FILE

Start/Finish Old Dungeon Ghyll Car Park (Pay and Display), GR 285061
Distance 13km (8 miles)
Height gain 945m (3100ft)
Walking time 6 hours
Type of walk A rugged, high mountain walk on cairned and well-trodden pathways, but confusing in poor visibility. The descent of Rossett Gill can be awkward in winter conditions

The Route in Brief

Start From the car park go to the main valley road, turn R to junction, and ahead down the access to Stool End Farm.
1 Through the farm, ascend R, on rising path on to The Band and continue to reach the Three Tarns col.
2 Climb R, up loose and steep path to summit of Bow Fell.
3 Start off N, then gradually swing round to W, to Ore Gap. Ascend Esk Pike.
4 Cross summit, and descend to Esk Hause.
5 Go R, heading down to Angle Tarn, and on down Rossett Gill.
6 Walk out through Mickleden to return to the Old Dungeon Ghyll Hotel.

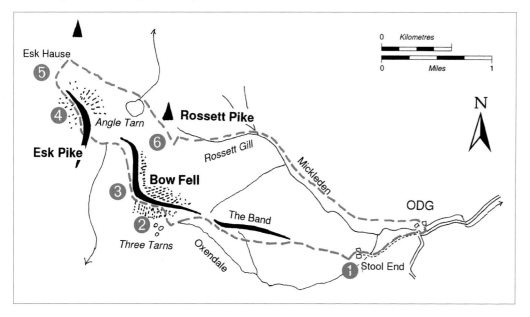

THE LANGDALE PIKES

Quite which 'pikes' actually comprise the Langdale Pikes is a moot point: Harrison Stickle and Pike of Stickle surely, but what of Loft Crag, Pavey Ark, Thunacar Knott, even Sergeant Man? Certainly it is the two former that stand out when seen across the top end of Windermere, so it is understandable why they must be included. It could be argued that the Langdale Pikes are only those 'pikes' that overlook 'Langdale' but then you must include Loft Crag, too. Or perhaps it is those that are logically ascended from Langdale; so now add Pavey Ark and Thunacar Knott. Thankfully, it is of no real consequence, other than for purists. This extended tour visits them all and throws in Sergeant Man for good measure. En route, you can discuss to your heart's content the merits of including each, but try to enjoy the superb walking as well.

Leave the New Dungeon Ghyll car park at its top end, on a path that darts through walls before setting off in earnest. At a fence gap, keep right to begin a steady ascent that is never far from Stickle Ghyll, a fine mountain stream that used to be called Mill Gill.

A wooden bridge allows a far easier crossing of the gill than in the former boulder-hopping days, and footpath restoration has greatly improved the ascent to one of Lakeland's most popular locations, Stickle Tarn. The path is never in doubt and passes some fine cascades when the gill is in spate. Gradually, as height is gained, the adjoining crags begin to close in a little. Some walkers prefer to cross the gill when this happens but there is an easy and fairly obvious way through the rocks and little advantage in avoiding them. Soon, the paths, for there is one on each side of the stream now, arrive at the serene expanse of Stickle Tarn (1), beneath the awe-inspiring cliffs of Pavey Ark – a stunning moment, even on the fiftieth experience.

Keeping the tarn to your left, follow a path going right, round the edge of the tarn. Bright Beck and other feeder streams confluence here, so there are damp moments as the path ambles towards the long, descending threshold of Blea Rigg. Once on this gentle ridge, follow it north-west to a brief dip just below Sergeant Man (2), from where the top is a quick scamper away.

Left: The Langdale Pikes and (right) viewed from Elterwater

As a viewpoint, Sergeant Man, whether or not embraced within the Langdale Pike Appellation Controllée, is especially fine. Both Pavey Ark and Harrison Pike are seen from an unusual angle, lounging against the backdrop of Wetherlam and the Coniston fells. The great parade of Fairfield, Helvellyn and the humpy Dodds range to the east, while westwards Crinkle Crags, Bow Fell and Great Gable gather around the edges.

Alas, northwards the panorama is spoiled by the unappetising blot of High White Stones, also known as High Raise. With time aplenty you can easily include it in the walk in twenty minutes of blatant peak-bagging but otherwise continue the circuit on a path curving west and south to pass over Thunacar Knott before visiting Pavey Ark.

The whole of the section from Sergeant Man to Harrison Stickle can be very confusing in poor visibility and though there is a continuous path, it is easily missed particularly among the rock outcrops that crown Pavey Ark and litter the ensuing stretch across to Harrison Stickle. The wisest course is to stick with the path and only deviate to visit nearby summits if visibility is good and you can see how to rejoin the path. In this way, you should eventually draw up beneath the final rocky cone of Harrison Stickle (3) and for a few minutes indulge in a little easy scrambling.

Pike of Stickle, Loft Crag and Harrison Stickle

The highest point, marked by one of many cairns, lies at the northern end of the neat summit plateau.

To continue to Pike of Stickle, go west down a prominent stony path to a boggy stretch of ground, feeding Dungeon Ghyll to the left. Keep ahead, bypassing Loft Crag, though on a clear day it is no hardship to include it. Paths run clearly on to the top of Pike of Stickle's enormous scree gully, a quick, but badly eroded and dangerous way down to Mickleden and **not** advised.

Cross the top of the gully and ascend the path to the top of the fell **(4)**. A breathtaking panorama awaits, overlooking Mickleden, The Band, Oxendale to Pike of Blisco, Crinkle Crag and Bow Fell; even Great Gable crowds in on the act, beyond Rossett Pike.

To continue, leave Pike of Stickle by the path you used to ascend it, then bear left (north-west) to follow a path across the grassy expanse of Martcrag Moor that meets the Cumbria Way at the top of Stake Pass **(5)**. Go left down Stake Gill towards the upper reaches of Mickleden, and once on level ground in the valley bottom, head left (south-east), still with the Cumbria Way, which will lead you to the Old Dungeon Ghyll Hotel. Just before the final gate, at the rear of the buildings, go left, above a wall and follow a stony track back to the start.

FACT FILE

Start/Finish National Trust car park, New Dungeon Ghyll, GR 295064
Distance 14km (8³/₄ miles)
Height gain 800m (2625ft)
Walking time 5–5¹/₂ hours
Type of walk A long and tiring circuit that should not be undertaken in poor visibility

The Route in Brief

Start Leave the New Dungeon Ghyll car park at the top end and follow the ascending path to Stickle Tarn.

1 Keep the tarn on your L and circle round to reach Blea Rigg, ascending from there to Sergeant Man.
2 Continue on curving path to Thunacar Knott, Pavey Ark (optional) and Harrison Stickle.
3 Descend W, cross boggy stretch to follow path to Pike of Stickle.
4 Descend Pike of Stickle and turn L (NW) across Martcrag Moor to top of Stake Pass.
5 Go L (SW), down Stake Gill to Mickleden, and L out of valley to Old Dungeon Ghyll, following path above wall to return to start.

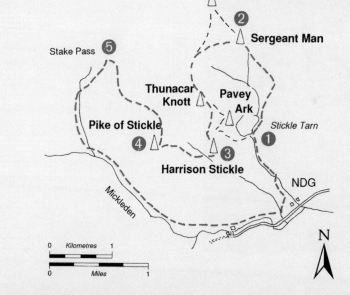

JACK'S RAKE AND HARRISON STICKLE

In days of derring-do, when rock climbing filled my weekends, I would romp up Jack's Rake on Pavey Ark in a trice; now I find I've changed my mind, I'm not so self-assured. Unquestionably one of the most famous lines in Britain, Jack's Rake is no place for walkers without scrambling ability; some would say it borders on a moderate rock climb, but there the argument becomes too subjective. Viewed from the safety of Sergeant Man it appears as little more than a wide ledge rising at a gentle angle across the steep face of the fell. Standing at the bottom, looking up, you face a rather different perspective. Certainly it is an outstanding scramble, the finest way to the top of Pavey Ark and a splendid challenge. In winter conditions it is alpine in nature and then *only* for experienced winter mountaineers.

Start from the National Trust car park at New Dungeon Ghyll and follow the path to Stickle Tarn (1), described in Walk 8. Circle left, round the tarn keeping fairly close to the water's edge at first and ignoring a rising path on the left that heads for Harrison Stickle. Gradually, you rise away from the tarn, and cross rough, bouldery ground to the foot of the Rake (2). If, on closer acquaintance, the Rake no longer holds any appeal, keep moving to the right and ascend Pavey Ark by the obvious Easy Gully, turning left at the top to reach the summit.

There is no problem route-finding on Jack's Rake, indeed there is no choice in the matter, and in spite of a steepish, wet start, you experience little sense of exposure because of the grooved nature of the Rake. Careful placing of hands and feet, and a little forethought in doing so, is the key both to success and to enjoying the ascent rather than suffering it.

There are rock climbs above and below the Rake, so try not to dislodge any rocks. Half way up you reach a small platform at the foot of an obvious rock chimney, Gwynne's Chimney, a suitable spot for a breather.

Continuing, a narrow rock gully ahead makes you think for a while about placement of hands and feet, beyond which pleasant scrambling leads across the more open top of Great Gully and an obvious line up and over slabs and rock knuckles, with the occasional awkward manoeuvre, before rising to meet a wall. Once you have reached the wall, circle round to the right to reach the summit of Pavey Ark (3), and its eyrie-like view.

Above: On the summit of Harrison Stickle
Opposite: Harrison Stickle from Jack's Rake

The continuation to Harrison Stickle begins by returning to the wall and following a cairned path across rough ground to the col between Pavey Ark and Harrison Stickle. In mist this can be confusing. The col is broad and studded with boulders and rock outcrops but through them a path probes Harrison Stickle's defences, finishing with a mild rocky flourish (avoidable) to reach the airy summit plateau **(4)**.

The return is made down the splendid ravine of Dungeon Ghyll, setting off from Harrison Stickle heading west, down a rock and scree path to a wide, grassy stretch from where a path goes ahead to Pike of Stickle, while the way down Dungeon Ghyll moves left, on a good path.

As you round the base of Harrison Stickle, you cross an area worked by Neolithic and early-Bronze Age Man for the 'rough-outs' from which they fashioned stone axes. Beyond this the stony terrain gives way to grass as the path descends to a small outlier, Pike How, an excellent vantage point to which you will need to divert briefly.

The on-going path descends to the right of Pike How before continuing down through bracken to the intake wall, where the path is deflected, right, before crossing the wall to traverse the intake fields to a gate not far above the New Dungeon Ghyll car park.

FACT FILE

Start/Finish National Trust car park, New Dungeon Ghyll, GR 295064
Distance 5.5km (3½ miles)
Height gain 650m (2130ft)
Walking time 4–5 hours
Type of walk A long uphill pull preludes a rocky scramble. Rough terrain throughout, with some confusion in poor visibility, when it is best avoided

The Route in Brief
Start Using the route described in Walk 8, ascend to Stickle Tarn.
1 Circle the tarn and ascend rough ground to the foot of Jack's Rake.
2 Ascend the Rake, turning R on meeting a wall at the top, to reach the summit.
3 Cross to Harrison Stickle.
4 Descend W to top of Dungeon Ghyll, and descend L, across rocks and then grass, bypassing Pike How, to return to the valley.

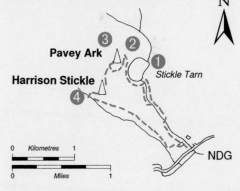

37

ALLEN CRAGS AND GLARAMARA

At the southern end of Borrowdale the valley divides and sends one arm past Stonethwaite and Eagle Crag and another down to Seathwaite and Stockley Bridge. Wedged between the two is a superbly long and craggy ridge that reaches south to Esk Hause and embraces two principal summits, Glaramara and Allen Crags. A complete traverse of this magnificent ridge is a major undertaking, inordinately satisfying and at its best in spring or autumn when the play of the light is at its most enchanting. Here the ridge is preceded by a long and steady approach via Seathwaite and Grains Gill to Esk Hause, where you turn tail and begin the long journey back. Mist makes the ridge, which is a company of rocky knolls, boggy hollows and tiny tarns, a place blessed with ample opportunity to go wrong so leave this walk for a fine, clear day. In winter sunshine it presents a superb outing on which an ice axe is essential and crampons desirable towards the end.

Left: Glaramara from the top of Ruddy Gill
Opposite: Allen Crags from Esk Hause

Begin from the car park at Seatoller and leave it, turning left down the road and keeping left as you pass the narrow lane to Seathwaite. For a speedier start you can use the lane to reach Seathwaite, but it is less hazardous to keep on as far as Strands Bridge, where a footpath to Seathwaite leaves the road at the access to Thorneythwaite Farm. This footpath is part of the Allerdale Ramble and continues past Thorneythwaite Farm to reach Seathwaite just beyond the farm buildings.

Turn left and follow the broad track away from the farm and onwards, parallel with the combined waters of Grains Gill and Styhead Gill, as far as Stockley Bridge (1). Cross the bridge, and at a gate turn left beside the wall, then follow the long and steadily rising path southwards with Glaramara directly above you on the left and the lower slopes of Seathwaite Fell on your right.

At the top of an obviously renovated footpath you reach a few level strides high above the ravine of Ruddy Gill. A quick dip takes you across the red-rock gulch to climb to a path linking Sty Head (right) with Esk Hause. Turn left on this path, beneath the glare of Great End. When it forks, take the lower branch and continue easily to Esk Hause (2).

From Esk Hause, Allen Crags (3) is easily

FACT FILE

Start/Finish Car park at Seatoller, GR 245138
Distance 13km (8 miles)
Height gain 820m (2690ft)
Walking time 5–6 hours
Type of walk A long and tough mountain walk, potentially confusing in misty conditions, when the section north of Glaramara should be abandoned in favour of a descent via Thorneythwaite Fell. Care needed on the steep final descent, especially in winter

The Route in Brief

Start Leave the Seatoller car park and walk down the road and round to Strands Bridge, there leaving the road for a track and path to Seathwaite Farm. Go L to Stockley Bridge.
1 Across the bridge go L at a gate and ascend along the line of Grains Gill to reach and cross Ruddy Gill. Go L and branch L, to Esk Hause.
2 Ascend Allen Crags.
3 Continue across hillocky terrain to Glaramara.
4 Head NE to pass Combe Head and reach Rosthwaite Fell.
5 Descend to Tarn at Leaves, and by Rottenstone Gill regain main path, followed out to Borrowdale road.

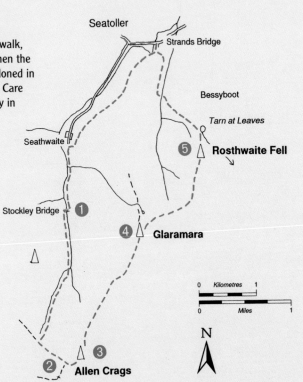

reached by a stony trod that curves up to the summit, and a grand view of the Langdale Pikes, Esk Pike, Bow Fell, and Great End.

The continuation to Glaramara pursues a stony path, passing a scattering of tiny tarns, some of which have names – High House Tarn and Lingcomb Tarns – and not a few minor summits, before you haul on to Glaramara's welcome top **(4)**.

As you continue roughly north-east from Glaramara a short rock step requires care, before you cross to another cluster of small tarns beneath Combe Head. A path begins descending immediately from Glaramara to curve around the west side of fell and over Thorneythwaite Fell. This is a possible variant way down and brings you into Combe Gill before running out to Strands Bridge. Otherwise, head slightly right of those tarns and take to steeper ground rising to the right of Combe Head, to reach a natural corridor, Combe Door.

A path crosses Combe Door and though it is indistinct you can use it to navigate round the wide hollow (Combe Gill) between Thorneythwaite Fell and Rosthwaite Fell, and so reach the summit of the latter, Rosthwaite Cam **(5)**, directly overlooking reed-laden Tarn at Leaves.

Continue by descending to the tarn, from where it is worth following the cairned path on to Bessyboot, a superb vantage point. Retrace your steps, then head west, down the easy red ravine of Rottenstone Gill, by steep grassy slopes to reach a path that crosses Combe Gill near a sheepfold before heading north to the Borrowdale road. Turn left to return to Seatoller.

WATENDLATH AND ULLSCARF

The ultimate objective of this walk is Ullscarf, an isolated, curmudgeonly fell that turns its back on everyone and surrounds itself with wet ground, as if actively discouraging visitors. Closer acquaintance reveals a broad grassy upland, buttressed by a ferocious display of crags, some highly regarded by rock climbers. On Ullscarf, a moorland oasis at the heart of rocky Lakeland, the scope for long striding days is considerable, the likelihood of getting wet feet, likewise.

You can reach Ullscarf quite easily from Wythburn or from Rosthwaite (via Stonethwaite), both routes approaching the summit over the boggy pass of Greenup Edge. But the circuit described here is an unashamed excuse to visit the attractive hamlet of Watendlath. Described by Dorothy Wordsworth as 'a heavenly scene', Watendlath is beautifully rustic, a tranquil setting today, but once a thoroughfare for packhorses in the days when most of the fells hereabouts were owned and farmed by Fountains Abbey, or that at Furness. Because it is attractive, and at the end of a fine drive, it is popular. So, chose your day with care; out of the tourist season, when the air is clear and bright.

Dock Tarn

Leave the car park and turn right (east), to ascend the adjacent fell, High Tove. The path, signposted Blea Tarn and Wythburn, sets you off through a gate, climbing zigzags that end where the intake wall turns south. This is the way to go, following a path across marshy ground that leads to Blea Tarn. The path is intermittently cairned, though the way is not in doubt. Eventually you reach a high point overlooking Blea Tarn (1), to which there is a short descent.

Keeping the tarn on your right follow the often wet shoreline path and continue in the same direction, rising now on a less prominent path, but one which is a long-established way to Wythburn. At its highest point, even if you go a little astray, you intersect a fenceline along the watershed.

The retrospective view of Blea Tarn is splendid; it occupies a moorland basin, held in place by morainic debris, with only the rising ground of Coldbarrow Fell to give shape to the scene. Beyond the dip that conceals Watendlath, the knobbles of heathery Grange Fell prelude those of Maiden Moor, High Spy and the North Western Fells.

South, along the fenceline rises Standing Crag (2), an obstruction that causes some thought before you can continue with the fence, across grassy and rather drier terrain. Soon, as you start ascending the slopes of Ullscarf, the fence expires, leaving you to continue with the remains of an older fence that eventually leads you south to the large cairn marking the top of the fell (3).

Pedants may quibble, but Ullscarf is commonly looked upon as the most central fell in the Lake District in excess of 610m (2000ft), a distinction that justifies your attention. When sufficiently impressed with your geographical significance, retrace your steps, but only until the fenceposts turn to the north-east. Now walk ahead, ignoring a new fence not yet shown on maps, to reach a cairn on High Saddle, an isolated outcrop. Press on, across Coldbarrow Fell to reach Low Saddle and a fine view of Blea Tarn, and a more distant one of your next objective, Dock Tarn.

The tarn disappears from sight as you descend towards it, so aim instead for a conspicuous cairn on a small hillock, Green Combe. Grass and easy walking give way to hungry heather that plucks at socks and boot-laces, a nuisance only marginally relieved as you descend from Green Combe to Dock Tarn (4).

In late summer and early autumn, the colours around Dock Tarn are at their most vibrant, for it is then that the heather is in full bloom, water lilies and swaying reeds brighten the tarn and dark green bracken clads the rock-punctuated surrounds. It is a memorable sight, beyond which, peering over a low col, Skiddaw muscles in on the act.

A good path runs along the western edge of the tarn, before descending, now marked by posts, to reach the intake fields around Watendlath, and a final few minutes descending gracefully to its tarn.

Right: Near Watendlath
Pages 44–5: Above Watendlath

Start/Finish Car park, Watendlath, GR 275163
Distance 10km (6¹/₄ miles)
Height gain 460m (1510ft)
Walking time 4–5 hours
Type of walk Moorland wandering, often boggy and enough uncertainty about paths to make this inadvisable in poor visibility

The Route in Brief

Start Leave the car park and turn R, ascending the signposted path towards High Tove, leaving this at the intake wall, to follow a signposted path to Blea Tarn.
1 Continue past tarn, rising to fence on watershed, N of Standing Crag. Follow fence to the crag.
2 Continue with fence, and then fenceposts to summit of Ullscarf.
3 Retrace steps a short way, N, then NNE, over High Saddle and Low Saddle to reach Green Combe and Dock Tarn.
4 Keep to path on W side of Dock Tarn, and head N, following waymarked path to intake above Watendlath, descending from there to the start.

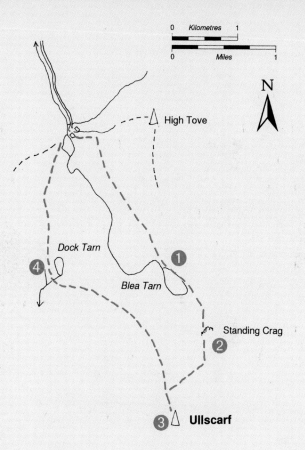

45

EASEDALE AND HELM CRAG

Far Easedale Gill

Hidden high among the folds of flowing fells, Easedale Tarn and its higher and smaller neighbour Codale Tarn have been places of popular pilgrimage since Victorian times. Nothing much has changed. With the fascination of Grasmere as a base and an easy approach, enlivened by the foaming cascades of Sourmilk Gill, the steady flow of visitors continues unabated. To the north-east, across the valley of Far Easedale, the imaginative forms of the Lion and the Lamb, Helm Crag's topmost rocks receive much the same attention, often with the added passage of those pursuing the Northern Coast to Coast Walk, bound for Robin Hood's Bay.

This circular walk embraces both tarn and crag, climbing out of Easedale on to the delightful Blea Rigg and rising to Sergeant Man, from whence the opportunity is taken to include High Raise, before returning to the head of Far Easedale and the long ridge of Helm Crag.

There are a number of car parks in Grasmere, any of them would be suitable as a starting point. The way out lies up Easedale Road, from the village centre, towards Goody Bridge. Keep going until you reach a footpath (signposted to Easedale Tarn), just at a bend. Cross Easedale Beck and continue towards the white splash of Sourmilk Gill which you can see ahead. The path climbs beside the gill and turns abruptly left at the head of the falls, then continues to Easedale Tarn **(1)**. This splendid oasis lies surrounded by bracken- and grass-clad hummocks, punctuated by the occasional rocky outcrop – Tarn Crag, Slapestone Edge and pyramidal Belles Knott.

Another rise leads up between Eagle Crag and Belles Knott, beside which the path forks. The right branch (not marked on maps) visits Codale Tarn, a worthwhile diversion, while the onward route lies to the left, continuing to climb steadily until Stickle Tarn, backed by Pavey Ark and Harrison Stickle, lies at your feet. Looking down into Easedale the landscape of rolling grey-green fells and dark blue tarns, backed by the bulging forms of Fairfield and the Helvellyn range, is at its best in autumn when the bracken lends a russet vibrancy to the scene.

With little ado the path continues north-west to Sergeant Man **(2)**, beyond which a grassy trod leads to the vast plateau of High Raise, descending slightly to reach Low White Stones. Heading now north-north-east, the path continues down to the boggy col of Greenup Edge (3), where it meets the Northern Coast to Coast Walk, its companion for the rest of the journey back to Grasmere.

A descending path now traverses a boggy shelf at the head of the Wyth Burn valley, running on to the col at the head of Far Easedale (4). From here, ignore the obvious descending path and pursue instead a prominent, narrow path that passes first round Calf Crag and then presses on to Gibson Knott. Laden with numerous ups and downs, the path rarely follows the crest of the ridge but is no less entertaining for that. With a sense of purpose it crosses a dip to Bracken Hause before concluding with a rugged little assault on the jumbled chaos that is the top of Helm Crag (5).

Many of the crazily angled crags up here have acquired names, including the highest point itself, which, for obvious reasons when you are close to it, is called the Howitzer. If to actually stand on a summit is the only way to say you have conquered it, you may find that Helm Crag gives you cause to reappraise the wisdom of such a precise condition – perhaps a simple pat on the head would do.

No amount of head scratching, however, can form the rocks into the familiar lion and its lamb: for that you need to be down below. Indeed, you pass them unknowingly as you leave the summit, descending to the extreme edge of the ridge to a steep slope and a path that zigzags to the valley bottom. A simple stroll out, along Easedale Road, is all that remains.

FACT FILE

Start/Finish Grasmere village, GR 337077
Distance 14km (8³/₄ miles)
Height gain 770m (2525ft)
Walking time 5–6 hours
Type of walk A long and overall rugged walk, visiting fells where clear visibility is essential. Finishes with a fine, rocky ridge and a steep descent

The Route in Brief
Start Leave Grasmere up Easedale Road, leaving it at a bend for a footpath signposted to Easedale

Tarn. Cross Easedale Beck and climb beside Sourmilk Gill to reach Easedale Tarn.

1 Continue past the tarn, with an optional diversion to Codale Tarn, before climbing on to Blea Rigg and ascending to Sergeant Man.

2 Cross grassy terrain to High Raise and descend first to Low White Stones and then Greenup Edge.

3 Traverse above Wyth Burn to reach the col at the head of Far Easedale.

4 Go L, around Calf Crag, to cross the long ridge to Helm Crag.

5 Descend steeply from Helm Crag to the valley floor, and follow Easedale Road back to Grasmere.

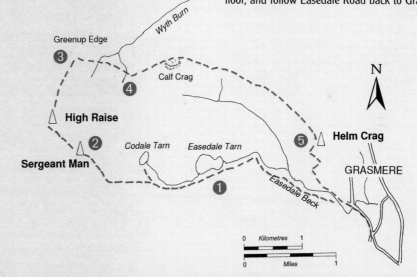

THE DODDS

Lacking crag-bound corries, soaring arêtes and dramatic profiles, the sprawling, rounded, grassy domes of the Dodds do not readily encourage closer acquaintance. They are formed from extensive lava flows, producing a bland plateau-like surface and wide-reaching moorlands. The Dodds lie at the northern end of a long ridge extending from Rydal Water at Nab Scar, across Fairfield and the Helvellyn range, and are separated from the latter by an ancient thoroughfare, the Sticks Pass.

I have an unhappy feeling that these days the Dodds are looked upon as no more than an unavoidable part of the Bob Graham Round, that massive twenty-four hour (or less) epic tour of Lakeland, or part of the greater ridge traverse, that by virtue of being there, have to be included. Few walkers, I suspect, visit the Dodds for their own intrinsic qualities which in spite of a sameness about the scenery include excellent, easy walking, good views and a moorland solitude that is second to none. True, that is not everyone's idea of Lakeland walking, but the Dodds are too high and too wide to be ignored and make their own contribution to the fell walking (and

skiing) repertoire of the Lake District, one that everyone should come to sample.

Those who like to study these things will notice that to the east the Dodds flow endlessly and smoothly down towards Ullswater in great moorland swathes that contrast remarkably with the dramatic ruggedness of the same eastern profiles of the Helvellyn and Fairfield ranges. Correspondingly, the steepness of the Dodds' western prospect, overlooking St John's in the Vale, is significantly different from the rounded posteriors that the higher ranges present to the west. From this, geologists may make deductions about glacial movements within the Lake District that will defeat the layman.

As you enter St John's in the Vale, at its southern portal rises an amazing heap of boulders known originally as Green Crag, a popular playground for the hard men of the rock-climbing world, but one steeped in poetic legend. These days it is known as Castle Rock and when viewed from a distance you can see why, for it does indeed look like the cast-down ruins of some medieval castle towering above the surrounding land in a position

of strategic prominence, seemingly impregnable.

With such ingredients it is not surprising that tales of mystery and intrigue have been heaped upon its craggy crown. Hutchinson, the Cumberland historian, commenting upon its lofty turrets and ragged battlements warned anyone who approached in the hope of finding a route into its secret ways that 'certain genii who govern the place, by virtue of their supernatural art and necromancy, will strip it of all its beauties, and, by enchantment, transform the magic walls'.

Never one to let a prospective tale of chivalry go by unpenned, Walter Scott transformed this legend into a long tale about King Arthur in *Bridal of Triermain*, since when the crag has been known as the Castle Rock of Triermain. It stands guardian at the entrance to the dale, which proves to be a pleasant and fertile thoroughfare, though more often used these days as a short cut to or from Penrith.

Around the northern edges of the Dodds an old coach road links Wanthwaite in St John's in the Vale with far off Dockray, and proves to be the means by which many an easy circuit of the fells may be accomplished.

Clough Head and the Castlerigg Stone Circle

SHEFFIELD PIKE

Sheffield Pike is not an attractive fell, more a scrappy gathering together of debris left over from the creation of Patterdale. Indeed, if primeval Patterdale had possessed a carpet, Sheffield Pike would have been swept under it. As it is, it rises as an untidy pile above two dales, Glenridding and Glencoynedale, and has not benefited from the attentions of nineteenth-century man, who plundered the fellsides for lead. Yet, seemingly against the odds, Sheffield Pike *does* have appeal, especially during the busy summer months and if you approach through Glencoyne Wood and loop round to ascend the south-east ridge.

Begin from the car park in Glenridding and leave it at its northern end on to the main road. Cross the road in a short while on to a permissive path along Ullswater's edge. As you approach Mossdale Bay (1), you cross inflowing Mossdale Beck and should then keep an eye open for a signposted track on the opposite side of the road, which

Sheffield Pike from the slopes of Gowbarrow Fell

ascends into Glencoyne Wood beside a wall.

The track rises past a row of cottages with the name Seldom Seen (2), built long ago to accommodate miners at the Greenside Mine. Beyond, the track ends and a path continues to a gate at a wall junction. Go through the gate and turn left, climbing beside a wall at the upper edge of Glencoyne Wood.

If you stick with the wall you will in time join the south-east ridge, but you will lose height in the process. Instead, as the wall starts going down, branch right and continue climbing, aiming just left of an iron boundary post on Heron Pike ahead. The post, which has a companion on the other side of the fell near Nick Head, marks the frontier between the Marshall Estate of Patterdale and the Howard Estate of Greystoke. The way is marked by a few small cairns and rises through heather and rocky outcrops to a good viewpoint overlooking Ullswater, Heron Pike (3).

Boggy ground lies ahead, occupying a small depression and an intermittent path across grass and heather, heading east of north to a prominent cairn on the slopes of Sheffield Pike. Further west is a larger cairn that marks the summit of the fell (4), a craggy affair dotted with small pools and cursed with numerous marshy hollows.

From the summit, head west to reach a conspicuous saddle, Nick Head. It is easy walking now but the view is marred by widespread mining spoil. When you reach a more prominent path, descend south-west to reach the higher levels of the Greenside Mine. Go down through the workings and marvel (or despair) at man's endeavour. Soon you arrive at the former mine buildings that now serve as a youth hostel (Helvellyn) and outdoor activities centre.

The Greenside Mine was first opened in the late eighteenth century but only became significantly productive in 1825. Before 1825 the mine was quite shallow and ore was taken over the Sticks Pass for smelting at Stoneycroft Ghyll in Newlands. In later years, the galena (lead ore) was smelted at the mine site, where up to twelve ounces of silver per ton was produced along with a yield of almost eighty per cent lead.

In spite of what we might think of the place today, the Greenside Mine brought considerable prosperity to Patterdale, its population increasing almost threefold in the fifty years following the turn of the century. By the end of the nineteenth century electrical winding gear was in use and electric engines were used underground for haulage, making Greenside the best-equipped mine in the Lake District.

From the youth hostel a broad track, unsurfaced, runs back down to the start at Glenridding.

FACT FILE

Start/Finish Glenridding car park, GR 386169
Distance 7km (4½ miles)
Height gain 520m (1705ft)
Walking time 3–3½ hours
Type of walk A strenuous walk over rough terrain

The Route in Brief

Start Walk N along the road from the Glenridding car park to reach a shore path heading for Mossdale Bay.

1 Once over Mossdale Beck, cross the road and follow a track into Glencoyne Wood, going round to Seldom Seen.

2 Continue W, beside a wall to a gate, and then L along a wall, branching R at the highest point and climbing to Heron Pike.

3 Keep rising, E of N, to cairn and then W to summit.

4 Go W to reach Nick Head and descend SW to mines, following road out to Glenridding.

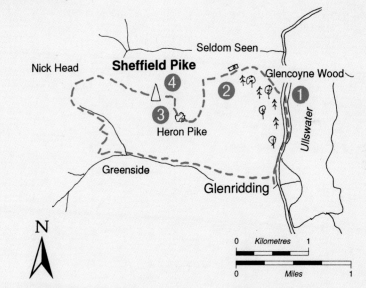

GREAT DODD FROM DOCKRAY

For such a massive area, the Dodds receive surprisingly few walkers. Tales of boggy, windswept, inhospitable moorland expanses abound and deter those without the patience to handle the peculiar problems this kind of terrain presents. True, navigation can be very difficult in bad visibility, and the occasional peat hag does claim the unwary passer-by, as one of my companions discovered when I first did this walk from Dockray. It was winter, the ground frozen solid, the snow crunching delightfully underfoot and the sun blazing from a clear blue sky, impotent against the bite of the sub-zero temperatures. My companion, a bank manager, to great applause and cheering, simply fell up to his armpits into a snow-filled hag during a moment of un-bank-manager-like frivolity; it was that kind of day. Wait for the same conditions and you will find this splendid circuit of the gathering grounds of Aira Force an immensely satisfying day out.

There is very limited parking in Dockray but if you ask permission at the Royal Hotel and return later for a drink or something to eat, you can park in the hotel car park; they welcome walkers at the Royal. Otherwise, you may have to drive along the minor road to High Row (you will have to walk it anyway), where you will find a small parking area.

The road runs along the north side of Aira Beck and you should follow it until, at a sharp bend, you can leave it by a gate near a sheepfold, at a signpost for Matterdale Common, the name for the vast area over which you are about to trek. For a few strides you travel the old coach road (1) that curls round the northern end of the Dodds to St John's in the Vale, but then leave this ancient thoroughfare for a grassy track.

Ahead of you, seemingly very far distant, rises the dome of Great Dodd, approached by a broad, ascending ridge that comprises a host of largely unidentifiable eminences with names like Horsemire Head, Low How, High Brow, Randerside and Lurgegill Head. High Brow stands out rather more than the rest and has a small cairn on it, from where you can gaze into the depths of Deepdale and onward to the heights that await.

Your next objective is the craggy lump of Randerside, beyond which you cross Lurgegill Head and start the brief, easy pull to Great Dodd summit (2), adorned by a cairn and a shelter some distance away. You need to visit the shelter en route to the next fell top, Watson's Dodd, and since it provides a better view than the summit cairn you may as well continue straight away and take a break there.

From the shelter, a grassy path heads southwest to meet a lower path arriving from Calfhow Pike, a rocky knoll north-west of Great Dodd. The ongoing path divides, with one branch missing Watson's Dodd altogether. Take the path heading to the right to reach Watson's Dodd, a seemingly dull and almost level platform beyond which, possibly to your surprise, the ground falls steeply to the southern end of St John's in the Vale and Thirlmere.

Now change direction again, heading southeast to rise on to Stybarrow Dodd (3), where a small cairn with a thick slab of slate projecting from it marks the summit. Onward the way starts off south-east down grassy slopes, with your target, Green Side (though modern maps call it White Stones), completely out of sight. A mid-course correction, going now east, soon brings you to the summit, a grassy expanse punctuated by low rocks.

Again a change of direction is needed as you

Great Dodd

FACT FILE

Start/Finish Dockray, GR 393216
Distance 15km (9½miles)
Height gain 725m (2380ft)
Walking time 5½–6 hours
Type of walk A long moorland walk, not recommended in poor visibility or after prolonged rain. Largely pathless, but easy walking

The Route in Brief

Start Leave Dockray along the lane beside Aira Beck and follow this to a sharp bend, where you leave the road for the old coach road.

1 Go through a gate and begin the long crossing of Matterdale Common, aiming for Great Dodd.
2 Continue SW to Watson's Dodd and SE to Stybarrow Dodd.
3 Head SE and E to Green Side (White Stones), and E of N to Hart Side.
4 Go SE to gap in wall, and then E over Brown Hills, curving NE to Swineside Knott and Common Fell. Route descends back to Dockray.

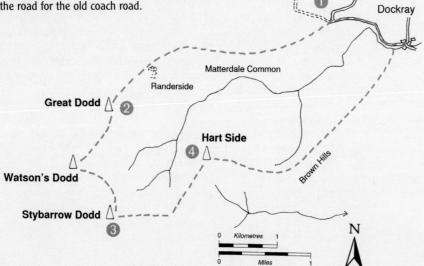

head for Hart Side, east of north, down a largely featureless slope to a group of summit cairns. The top of Hart Side **(4)** is marked by a curious man-made ditch, probably constructed by miners at Greenside, though with no evident reason.

More convoluted navigation turns you south-east once more as you head for the broad, grassy ridges of Watermillock Common. To the south the ground falls very steeply to Glencoynedale, but keep above this, targeting a gap in a wall just west of Brown Hills. Rough, trying, virtually trackless tussocky going now leads on over Swineside Knott to Common Fell, but it is along this final stretch that you will find arguably the finest view of Ullswater, a spectacle that makes the whole outing worthwhile, and might just lighten your stride.

More grassy slopes run on down to Dockray, crossing Pounder Sike, to reach a walled lane, ending at the A5091. Turn left along the road to return to the Royal Hotel. Walkers who elected to start from High Row still have some walking to do, all uphill.

CLOUGH HEAD AND GREAT DODD

Anyone approaching Clough Head from the south through St John's in the Vale may well be excused for forming the impression that the fell is impregnable, for the long line of crags that prevails on your right seems just that. Yet there are two ways through the crags and an easy alternative that creeps around the back from an old coach road linking Dockray and Wanthwaite. This walk takes one of the rough options to begin with, before striding along the northern end of the broad, grassy Dodds ridge to its highest point, from where trackless moorland wandering brings you down to the safety of the coach road.

Begin from Wanthwaite along the start of the old coach road (signposted: Matterdale Unsuitable for Motors) and continue past Hill Top Farm. When the track forks, keep left. When the track changes direction to head north, at the end of a stone wall, cross the fence on the right by a step-stile, near a small group of trees. Climb steeply on a distinct path through quarry spoil to reach the trackbed of an old mineral line, and go up the left edge of a quarry to another fence/stile. Continue to a ladder stile over the

Along the Old Coach Road, below Clough Head

intake wall, with the steep open fellside of Wanthwaite Bank rising above.

A shallow runnel grooves across the slope and continues as a grassy path rising in zigzags across Red Screes, the steep northern face of Clough Head. Finally the comfort of firm grass is gained at a small cairn south-west of the summit. Easy grass slopes lead east-north-east to the trig (1), and a fabulous view across the dale to the sculpted southern aspect of Blencathra, surely one of the most memorable sights in the Lake District.

Easy walking now follows, all the hard work is done and on a fine summer's day you can languish over the rest of the day. The next objective is Calfhow Pike, a neat oasis of rock set in a desert of grass, to which a broad and often wet path makes a direct line.

Onward the main path continues to Little Dodd but then skirts around the top of Millgill Head, avoiding the main summit. I can understand why walkers might elect to bypass Calfhow Pike but it beats me why anyone would choose to pass round the highest summit in the range. Of course, you won't, because you have to cross Great Dodd to begin the return journey.

The route back begins from the cairn at the northern edge of Great

Dodd (2), but if you want a break this offers no real shelter, so you should continue south-east for about 200m/yd where you will find a shelter with quite a pleasant view.

From the northern cairn, descend north-east on a straightforward path to the cairns on Randerside (3), and press on down the path until (at any time) you can launch yourself roughly northwards, targeting the western end of Wolf Crags, across grassy and invariably wet ground. Once round Wolf Crags (4) you soon reach the old coach road, near Mosedale Beck, and when you do simply turn left to follow this ancient highway all the way back to Wanthwaite, a very relaxed conclusion with excellent views of Blencathra.

The summit of Clough Head: Blencathra in the background

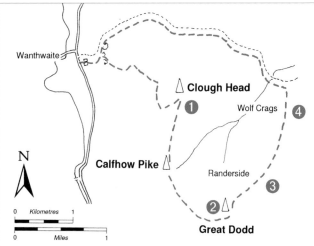

FACT FILE

Start/Finish Wanthwaite (limited parking near road junction), GR 316231
Distance 12km (7½ miles)
Height gain 870m (2855ft)
Walking time 5–5½ hours
Type of walk A rough and steep start precedes easy grassy walking. Not ideal in poor visibility

The Route in Brief
Start Leave Wanthwaite on a signposted track for Matterdale and continue past Hill Top Farm, to climb through quarry spoil to Wanthwaite Bank. Continue on a signposted path, in zigzags, across scree slopes to reach the grassy top of the crags. Ascend ENE to Clough Head.
1 Descend W of S to reach the rocky tor of Calfhow Pike and continue on a grassy track to Great Dodd.
2 Leave Great Dodd at its northern end, descending a path to Randerside.
3 Keep going down the path until (at any time) you can head north over trackless ground to the western edge of Wolf Crags.
4 Go past Wolf Crags to reach the old coach road, and turn L to follow it back to Wanthwaite.

HELVELLYN

The ascent of Helvellyn has been a challenge for adventurous spirits since the close of the eighteenth century, while the scramble across Striding Edge is probably the most popular day's outing in the Lake District; whether all plans to cross it are fulfilled is another matter.

The range is part of a great barrier between Ullswater to the east and Thirlmere, and lies between the Dodds to the north and the Fairfield range. Helvellyn, the highest point, lies roughly in the middle of this elongated ridge and is flanked by fells that require only small amounts of re-ascent. Along the top of the range where close-cropped grass and rocks prevail, the going is excellent, the whole of it traversed by a broad trail that can be joined at Grisedale Tarn and abandoned at the Sticks Pass. In between lie six major summits, seven if you include High Crag which has only a small amount of re-ascent and is not generally regarded as a separate mountain by those who require exactitude and minimum qualifications for their hills.

Viewed from the west you would be forgiven for thinking Helvellyn and its neighbours hold little appeal; the bare slopes bearing down on Thirlmere are extremely dull and offer only tiring ascents and there are no distinctive peaks to home in on. Yet the contrast with its eastern prospect could not be more marked, for here long-retreated glaciers have gouged great hollows in the Borrowdale Volcanic rocks. Scalloped corries, craggy cliffs, scree slopes, rocky glacis and narrow, pinnacled ridges rise in profusion and create a landscape that inspires every fell walker and frustrates more than a few, for everyone comes here sooner or later to try their feet at the classic round of Striding Edge and Swirral Edge. The Victorians did much the same, though they were able to hire ponies to carry them as far as Red Tarn, from where, ponies tethered to wait patiently, the edges and Helvellyn were assaulted.

Between Helvellyn and Dollywaggon Pike runs a splendid escarpment above glaciated corries and on a clear summer's day there is no finer walk than to follow this spectacular edge; winter, however, brings new dimensions that counsel against such an idea.

In spite of the popularity of the range and the hordes of ambitious pedestrians it produces, the opportunity still exists for the diligent map-reader to find quiet places away from the multitudes, which I shall leave you to discover for yourselves. And there are splendid low-level walks that take you into Grisedale, to the Greenside Mine above Glenridding and into Glencoyne-dale, as well as along the shores of Ullswater.

Above: On the long haul to the 'Hole in the Wall' (Striding Edge)
Opposite: Catstye Cam and Keppel Cove

STRIDING EDGE AND SWIRRAL EDGE

Possessing the capacity both to inspire and to traumatise, this classic ascent of Helvellyn, making use of the mountain's two eastern arms, may well be the most popular outing in the Lake District. Its acclaim draws every fell-walking ambition sooner or later, and thwarts more than a few. Technically the walk is not difficult but the sense of exposure is in places a little intimidating; under the cover of snow and ice it requires a good standard of winter expertise. During the rest of the year, all the real difficulties can be avoided.

The walk begins from Patterdale, where parking may be found at a number of places, and follows the main road past the church, leaving it at the first opportunity, at a bend, turning left along a side road leading past Patterdale Hall and ultimately into Grisedale. Follow the road as it bends right and tackle a short uphill section that ends just after a cottage.

Birks, a satellite of St Sunday Crag, rises steeply on the left, while an attractive and ornithologically interesting copse, flanking Grisedale Beck, lies over a wall on the right. When the wall ends the ground falls away to the beck in one of its most pleasant stretches. Follow the surfaced roadway, and at (but not through) a gate (1) leading to the farms at Braesteads and Elmhow, continue right, descending gently to cross Grisedale Beck by a bridge. Stay with the lane for a short distance further, until at a bend you leave through a small gate, to ascend a steep pasture to another gate and wall.

Beyond the gate, the path, here joined by a path from Glenridding (an alternative but steeper route), goes left and immediately forks. The lower branch sets off into Grisedale, while the higher (the route to be taken) begins the long and gradually rising approach to Striding Edge. As you climb, the view of Grisedale below becomes more and more impressive, brought abruptly to a halt by the crags of Nethermost Pike and Dollywaggon Pike that rise darkly at the head of the dale.

After a steady ascent of 2km (1¼ miles), the path, hitherto firm underfoot, becomes more broken, spreading in a broad spill of loose stones that heralds the Hole in the Wall (2), a stiled gap denoting the start of Striding Edge. Beyond the stile, a few scattered rocks overlooking Grisedale offer a tempting and justifiable excuse for a break. It is here that Helvellyn and its neighbour Catstyecam first come into view, above the basin that houses Red Tarn.

Striding Edge ripples along the left-hand edge of the hollow and when ready you follow an easy path heading towards it. Those with no problem with heights should consider leaving the main path to follow the crest of the approaching ridge; it gives splendid views of Grisedale and St Sunday Crag. Eventually, both this approach and the path join at the start of the Edge proper. From this point, anyone who is uncomfortable in exposed situations should locate a path, low down on the Red Tarn side, by means of which you can circumvent all the difficulties of the Edge. The rest begin by working a way round the right edge of the rocky buttress immediately ahead, beyond which an assortment of precarious paths thread the rocks of Striding Edge. Those with a head for heights will follow the very crest of this splendid arête; anyone less confident can still enjoy Striding Edge without too much commitment to exposed situations. Escape routes generally lie down on the right (Red Tarn side), as you move towards Helvellyn.

Towards the end of the Edge, the path directs you, rather awkwardly for a stride or two, to the top of a short descending gully. This is most easily descended by facing inwards; there are plenty of good hand- and footholds, and the difficulties more imagined than real. The whole of this final section can

Right: Striding Edge
Opposite: Descending the awkward gully at the end of Striding Edge

FACT FILE

Start/Finish Patterdale, GR 394161. Limited parking near memorial hut; car park near hotel. Road-side parking near entrance to Patterdale Hall, but avoid causing obstruction

Distance 12km (7½ miles)

Height gain 800m (2625ft)

Walking time 5–6 hours

Type of walk A high mountain undertaking requiring scrambling ability. Some exposure on Striding Edge (mostly avoidable) and Swirral Edge (not avoidable). A good head for heights would be useful. Serious winter undertaking, calling for experience and winter skills

The Route in Brief

Start Leave Patterdale and take the road past Patterdale Hall, ascending lane to reach gated entrance to Grisedale.

1 Turn R and cross Grisedale Beck, climbing to gate, and then by pasture to wall/gate. Turn L to follow higher path to Hole in the Wall.

2 Follow track to Striding Edge and follow the ridge (scrambling required at the end, below final pull to the top of Helvellyn).

3 Locate top of Swirral Edge and descend with care, to reach branching path, cutting R, across hollow containing Red Tarn, to rejoin outward route at the Hole in the Wall.

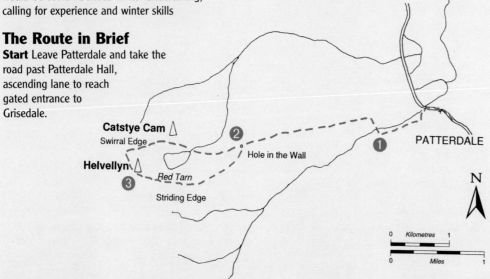

be avoided, however, on the side overlooking Nethermost Cove, but involves some descent that has to be regained.

Once beyond this brief scramble, all that remains is the bulging shoulder of Helvellyn. A little more, easy scrambling awaits as the ongoing route climbs in two large steps (avoid going too far to the right) to the edge of the summit plateau. A nearby memorial, overlooking Red Tarn, commemorates Charles Gough of Manchester, and his faithful dog.

The summit of Helvellyn **(3)** is something of an anticlimax. A cross-shelter provides some comfort from most winds and beyond it a short step up leads to the highest point, held in place by a lonely trig point.

Cross the top of the mountain and locate a low cairn at the top of Swirral Edge. The start of the descent is loose and exposed and in winter a hazardous spot. The frequent use of hands and bottoms will assist passage down Swirral Edge, but haste is *not* a good idea here. Eventually, all the rock work ends, as paths (on the Red Tarn side) combine to run ahead and up Catstyecam. This sentinel is a good vantage point and worth the brief detour.

From the col between Catstyecam and Swirral Edge, a branching path heads down, right, towards the outflowing stream of Red Tarn. A boggy interlude is experienced either side of the stream, before a slanting track runs left through tussocky grass, heading back to the Hole in the Wall, from where you can simply retrace your outward steps.

HELVELLYN TO DOLLYWAGGON PIKE

Well-suited to an ascent at any time of the year, this high mountain tour of the Helvellyn massif is especially ideal for good winter conditions, providing you take great care along the eastern rim, which can and does become heavily corniced. To complete this walk in times gone by you would need to spend an unacceptable amount of time road walking; now a splendid permissive path runs through the wooded slopes on the east side of Thirlmere, providing an easy conclusion.

Begin from the Swirls (North West Water) car park near Thirlspot, beside the A595, by taking the path from the rear of the parking area to engage the steep slopes of Helvellyn's north-west ridge, following the line of Helvellyn Gill. The way, which is never in doubt, is always steep and steepens even more as you approach Browncove Crags. Thankfully, this signifies that the end is close, for just above the crags the gradient eases.

The main path passes south of Lower Man, so leave it to take in this important satellite, continuing south to a brief dip where you rejoin the main path to climb on to the flat, stony plateau of Helvellyn. Go past the trig pillar to a small but significant rocky rise just overlooking the four-way shelter below: this slight elevation is the true summit of the mountain (1).

Press on past the shelter and down the broad track that follows, pausing for a moment at a small memorial to Bert Hinkler and John Leeming who on the 22 December 1926 landed a two-seater aircraft on the summit of Helvellyn, and, presumably, took off again. The track descends to a col, Swallow Scarth (2), where it forks. To the right and down, lies the means of abbreviating the walk, if necessary, by descending towards Wythburn until you intersect the Swirls Forest Trail, and there turning right to return to the car park.

The way to go lies ahead and you climb on to the edge of Nethermost Pike, with the ongoing path missing all the fun of a tour along the eastern rim of this southern end of the Helvellyn massif. In poor visibility, or heavily corniced conditions, keep to the path; it is a reliable guide. The edge route, however, provides successive outstanding views of Striding Edge and into Nethermost Cove and Ruthwaite Cove, and leads you over High Crag to Dollywaggon Pike. This is by far a more entertaining route.

From Dollywaggon Pike you need to rejoin the main path for a zigzagging descent that cares nothing for ageing knees, to reach Grisedale Tarn (3). It was into the tarn that a king of Strathclyde, Duvenald (corrupted to Dunmail), is said to have ceremoniously cast his crown, ridding himself of the insignia of office before setting off on pilgrimage.

Without descending all the way to the tarn (unless you want a break, for which it is ideally suited), bear right to a path above its northern shore to cross the threshold, once the boundary between Cumberland and Westmorland, to the north of Seat Sandal. Anyone who has yet to 'bag' Seat Sandal, and has the energy to do so, should tackle it now, ascending south by a dilapidated wall. It won't take long.

Otherwise, continue west, descending in company with Raise Beck towards Dunmail Raise (4). At the highest point of Dunmail Raise, apart from a modern dual carriageway, there stands a huge pile of stone, said to have been formed by Edmund I (AD939–46), to commemorate his defeat of King Duvenald. It has been suggested that the cairn covers the body of the king but the reality is that he, whether vanquished or not, continued to rule Strathclyde for some years before dying on pilgrimage in Rome.

Just above Dunmail Raise a gate leads through a wall to Homesdale Green Bridge across Birkside Gill. It continues with little variation in height through the conifers, crossing the Wythburn ascent path – where anyone taking the short cut from Swallow Scarth will arrive – and on over Whelpside Gill, before running out of the trees at the car park.

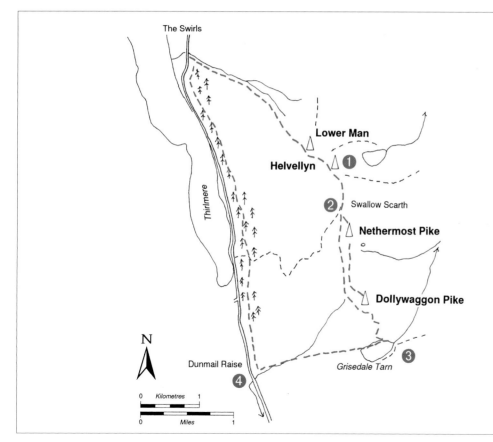

The Swirls

Lower Man

Helvellyn

Thirlmere

Swallow Scarth

Nethermost Pike

Dollywaggon Pike

Dunmail Raise

Grisedale Tarn

N

0   Kilometres   1

0   Miles   1

FACT FILE

Start/Finish The Swirls car park, GR 317169
Distance 14km (8³/₄ miles)
Height gain 890m (2920ft)
Walking time 5 hours
Type of walk A steep start leads to easy, high-level walking on good paths, finishing with a forest trail

The Route in Brief

Start Leave the rear of the car park and ascend steeply by a clear path to the top of Browncove Crags. Divert to include Lower Man, before continuing to the top of Helvellyn.
1 Continue S on a broad track to Swallow Scarth. (Escape route R, to Wythburn.)
2 Either follow continuing track around Nethermost Pike and Dollywaggon Pike to descend steeply to Grisedale Tarn, or climb L to follow escarpment rim, rejoining main path below Dollywaggon Pike, to descend to tarn.
3 Go W and descend by Raise Beck to Dunmail Raise.
4 Go R, through gate in wall and enter woodland, following clear forest trail back to the Swirls car park.

Left: Nethermost Pike and High Crag

RAISE, WHITE SIDE AND HELVELLYN

Thought originally to have taken its name from the practice of placing stakes as waymarkers across often mist-shrouded high ground, Sticks Pass is the way lead ore used to be brought during the nineteenth century from the Greenside Mine in Glenridding to smelters in Newlands. It may well have seen service, too, as an invasion route by marauding Scots bound for Patterdale. These days the only raiding it sees is that of walkers bagging the summits at the northern end of the Helvellyn massif, Raise and White Side. It is also a less populous route to Helvellyn itself.

A permissive path now links the car park at the foot of Helvellyn Gill with Stanah but this walk concludes by a more traditional route down the grassy flanks of White Side, only meeting the path in its later stages.

From Stanah take the lane (signposted to Glenridding via the Sticks Pass), climbing to a stile over a wall. Another stile leads you across a leat, shunting water to

Swirling mist over Raise and White Side

Thirlmere, beyond which a gate gives access to a bridge over Stanah Gill.

With the cascading gill to your left, climb through intake fields to a derelict sheepfold where the steep gradient finally relents. The sudden height gain brings its rewards in the form of outstanding views of Thirlmere and along St John's in the Vale to Blencathra, while a few minutes spent recovering your breath allows the magnificence of a landscape, here so often hurried by on the road below, to penetrate. Across the reservoir the wooded slopes rise to Ullscarf, while further south the probing dale of Wyth Burn leads the eye round to the shapely summit of Steel Fell above Dunmail Raise.

Resuming the walk you traverse a high grassy hollow, then branch right towards Sticks Gill, at the top of which a short pull brings you to Sticks Pass (1). Now a change of direction takes you south on a clear path to the rocky top of Raise, and on again, around the top of Keppel Cove to White Side (2), all delightfully easy walking.

Ahead the corries of Helvellyn and Lower Man await, a dramatic and rugged landscape that draws you on to tackle the abrupt, stony slopes of Lower Man, followed by a brief descent and re-ascent to gain the flat summit of Helvellyn (3) itself near the top of Swirral Edge.

Leave Helvellyn by returning over Lower Man and down the path to its lowest point before it climbs again to White Side. Just here,

branch left on an indistinct but improving path that flanks around the western slopes of White Side to reach a small rocky outcrop, Brown Crag (4).

Beyond Brown Crag the path steepens as it drops through bracken to a wall, where you meet up with the permissive path from Swirls. Turn right along this and cross Fisherplace Gill, keeping on to recross Stanah Gill at the foot of the Sticks Pass, from where the starting point is soon reached.

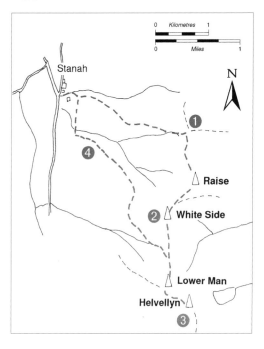

FACT FILE

Start/Finish Stanah, GR 318189 (limited parking)
Distance 11.5km (7 miles)
Height gain 945m (3100ft)
Walking time 4½–5 hours
Type of walk A high-level mountain walk on good paths

The Route in Brief

Start Leave Stanah along the lane signposted to Glenridding via the Sticks Pass, and ascend steeply at first, and then more easily, to the top of the Sticks Pass.
1 Turn S on a rising path to cross Raise and then SW to White Side.
2 Continue S to ascend Lower Man and continue to Helvellyn.
3 Return over Lower Man to its col with White Side and branch left on an indistinct path flanking to the W of White Side, and down to Brown Crag.
4 Continue steeply down to reach a wall, and turn R to return to Stanah Gill and the line of ascent.

5

FAIRFIELD AND AMBLESIDE

In the same way that Skiddaw dominates Keswick, so the domed presence of Fairfield, lying at the head of Rydal Beck, gazes down on the town of Ambleside. On either side of Rydal Beck, great embracing arms are flung southwards to the town as if craving your attention while offering obvious ways to the top of the mountain.

The main circuit of the horseshoe is splendid but is in normal conditions tame when compared with the remarkable glaciated valleys of Deepdale, Dovedale, Scandale and Grisedale, for here you find some of the most extravagantly wild and inviting fellscapes in Lakeland. Splendid days of wandering can be fashioned from these dales alone, seldom venturing on to the tops combining exciting valley approaches and rugged summits – the recipe is one that gives pure enjoyment.

While tramping around the Fairfield Horseshoe taking pictures for this book armed only with a flask of coffee and a few sandwiches, I recalled the tale I told in *The Lake Mountains* – Hodder and Stoughton (1987) but now out of print – of four walkers who more than a hundred years ago came from Manchester to tackle Fairfield by night. They brought with them 'thirty-six bottles of bitter beer, two bottles of gin, two bottles of sherry, one gallon of water, four loaves of bread, one leg of lamb, one leg of mutton, two fowls, one tongue, half-pound cigars, four carriage-lamps, and two packs of playing cards. [They] had also a large tent, which was borne on the back of a horse'. As I swilled down the last of my sandwiches with the last of my coffee, I looked down from the slopes of Nab Scar to the distant lights of Ambleside and wondered: things don't always change for the better!

Everyone will want to tackle Fairfield, of course, perhaps quite rightly to complete the horseshoe, but it is from the flanks, both east and west, that the most interesting ascents will be made. Dovedale, for example, is one of the most idyllic valleys, rising to the rock gymnasts' arena of Dove Crag, while neighbouring Deepdale is as rugged a valley as they come, and concludes in the cliffs of Hutaple Crag and Scrubby Crag. Less well known perhaps is Scandale, coursed by Scandale Beck and crossing, close by Little Hart Crag, into the splendid side dale of Caiston Glen.

Nor should you overlook the fine ascent to Fairfield that is possible from the northern end of Grasmere, taking an old packhorse route to Grisedale Hause before a loose haul to the summit. Closer still to Grasmere, an approach over Stone Arthur is not often contemplated, a fact that merely reflects the idiom that often we do not see the wood for the trees.

Anyone who crosses the Kirkstone Pass cannot fail to notice the battalion of crags and scree-ridden slopes that surround Red Screes. Standing apart from the main Fairfield group, Red Screes compares favourably with its siblings and is quite easily, if demandingly, ascended from Kirkstone Pass. An easier way is to ascend Caiston Glen to the head of Scandale and climb up from there, so avoiding the screes.

Out on a limb, but in its own way dominating Ambleside just as much as Fairfield, diminutive Wansfell Pike offers a magnificent circuit for a poor weather day, combining a fine vantage point with a trip into Troutbeck and a pleasant woodland conclusion.

Yes – if something different is what you seek, investigate the many nooks and crannies of Fairfield and its companions.

The Fairfield Group from Hartsop Dodd

STONE ARTHUR, FAIRFIELD AND SEAT SANDAL

Having no place in Arthurian legend other than that fuelled by romantic imagination, Stone Arthur is a prominent rock outcrop on a steep ridge, rising above Greenhead Gill, that links with the Fairfield Horseshoe just south of Great Rigg. Heroic deeds may, however, be needed to reach it, since its conquest involves an energetic pull of 425m (1395ft) in little over 1km (less than ¹/₂ a mile), with another 265m (870ft) waiting above, before you finally gasp on to the main ridge. Clearly, this is no route for idle curiosity. With markedly less effort, it continues over Fairfield and throws in a simple ascent of Seat Sandal for good measure.

Start in the village of Grasmere, from any car park in which you can find space. Leave the centre, going north along the B5287 to meet the main road, the A591 opposite The Swan Hotel (1). Walk up the lane beside The Swan to the second turning on the right (signposted to Greenhead Gill and Alcock Tarn). At the end you reach the open fell, where a path to Stone Arthur climbs steeply, close by a wall to the top of a small copse. The path now swings right, crosses a small stream and pursues the remains of a wall through extensive bracken and across the fall of the slope to reach the ridge descending from Stone Arthur, beyond which lies Greenhead Gill. Now turn left, and plod uphill to the rocky ramparts of Stone Arthur (2). You will need a rest, so turn around and admire the distant view into Easedale, where dark-eyed Easedale Tarn reposes peacefully amid encircling fells.

Procrastination being what it is, resume your upward tread, past a small stone shelter, and now ascend grassy slopes punctuated with small outcrops, to haul on to the main Fairfield Horseshoe ridge at a large cairn just south of Great Rigg (3). Within a few strides you can be perched, gathering your breath, high above Rydal Beck, and looking across to the long descending ridge of Dove Crag, High Pike and Low Pike. Northwards you might just pick out Striding Edge, poking its nose through a gap beyond Fairfield.

The next objective, Fairfield itself, is reached by a rocky rise across Great Rigg, and a much kinder slope to the broad, stony summit (4), adorned by a multiplicity of cairns and shelters. The best views are from the top of the north-eastern cliffs overlooking Gawk Cove and the upper reaches of Deepdale, close to which care is needed, particularly in winter conditions.

Due west of the summit cairn, a stony track leads on a steep descent to a dilapidated wall and down to Grisedale Hause. To the north Dollywaggon Pike towers over Grisedale Tarn, set in a wide boggy bowl – a place to which you can make a courtesy visit by turning right on reaching Grisedale Hause.

From the Hause you can ascend Seat Sandal directly by a steep but brief path. The summit (5) is a pleasant place to relax on a warm day, sufficiently distanced from the throngs of summer to give the illusion, if not the reality, of having the place to yourself.

Return to Grisedale Hause and turn right. A shallow hollow, Hause Moss, lies just below the col and may well have held a small tarn in

Great Rigg Man and Fairfield

FACT FILE

Start/Finish Grasmere village, GR 337077
Distance 12.5km (7¾ miles)
Height gain 980m (3215ft)
Walking time 5–6 hours
Type of walk Very steep climbing to grassy ridge and rocky summit that can be confusing in mist. A steep stony descent leads to a minor summit (optional), and a good path down to the valley, finishing on a quiet back road

The Route in Brief

Start Leave the centre of Grasmere heading N on the B-road to meet the A591, opposite The Swan Hotel.
1 Go along lane beside The Swan and take second turning on R to reach open fell. Climb L beside wall and then slant across fellside, through bracken, to reach ridge below Stone Arthur. Ascend steeply to Stone Arthur.
2 Continue up more steep slopes to gain main Fairfield Horseshoe ridge, near Great Rigg.
3 Go over Great Rigg and up easier slopes to Fairfield summit.
4 Descend W, steeply, to Grisedale Hause and ascend Seat Sandal.
5 Return to Hause and turn R, descending until path divides, and then go L, across stream to follow good path curving down above Tongue Gill to sheepfold at base. Go down walled lane to Mill Bridge.
6 Cross main road and go ahead on lane to Low Mill Bridge. Turn L and keep on to Goody Bridge. Turn L again, along Easedale Road, to return to Grasmere.

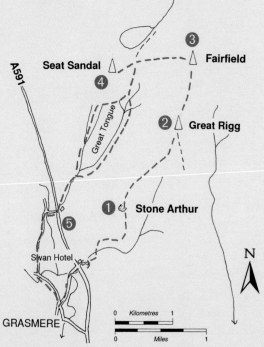

times gone by. Follow the path descending from the Hause until, just beyond Hause Moss, the path divides. Here you can cross the stream on your left and descend a broad rock step on wide ledges to gain a curving footpath that gives a splendid view of the waterfalls at the head of Tongue Gill. If you decide not to cross the stream, you can just as easily descend by Little Tongue Gill, the route used by Victorian travellers to reach the summit of Helvellyn on ponies. But this way is a little less interesting and gives a diminished view of the waterfalls. Both routes combine near a footbridge at the southern tip of Great Tongue, that wedge of ground that separates the two Tongue Gills.

Go ahead past sheep enclosures and descend to a gate and a walled path running down past cottages to the main road at Mill Bridge (**6**). You can speed down the A591 if you are in a hurry to return to Grasmere. Otherwise, cross the road and take a minor road ahead leading round to Low Mill Bridge, spanning the River Rothay. Here turn left on a back road past Thorney How Youth Hostel to reach Goody Bridge. Turn left again and follow Easedale Road back to the centre of Grasmere.

THE FAIRFIELD HORSESHOE

As a universal favourite, this classic walk would be rather less inspiring if it was known as the Rydal Beck Horseshoe; yet such it is, forming a complete, if elongated horseshoe around an attractive but generally disregarded mountain stream. Fairfield, on the other hand, features in a number of other horseshoe permutations, though none more commanding than the obvious challenge that faces any fell walker roaming the streets of Ambleside. Each year iron-lunged, steel-legged fell runners race clockwise round the horseshoe with varying degrees of anguish chiselled into their faces. This circuit takes an infinitely more leisurely approach, preferring an anti-clockwise round that avoids the too convenient distractions of Rydal Mount, one of Wordsworth's homes, until the end of the day.

A large car park at the northern end of Ambleside is an ideal starting point, but one that fills up quickly during the tourist season. Leave it and cross the main road to walk up Kirkstone Road opposite. Turn immediately left up Nook Lane, rising pleasantly to Nook End Farm. Here the lane becomes a

The head of the Fairfield Horseshoe

track and swings right to cross Scandale Beck at Low Sweden Bridge **(1)**, where the beck cascades through a wooded ravine.

As you cross the bridge and stroll up through green pastures, so the long ascending ridge leading northwards over Low Pike and High Pike begins to take shape. Purists will seek out a path that ascends beside the ridge wall, posing occasional rocky problems on the way. For the rest, a comfortable, ambling path keeps a distance from the wall until it reaches Low and High Brock Crags, a double barrier of rocks that often provides a period of calm on a windy day. Here the two routes rejoin to march on towards Low Pike, the first summit of the day. If you stick to the path, however, you will bypass Low Pike's summit, but having done so simply double-back, beside the wall, to reach the top. It is worth this brief diversion, for the summit is a good viewpoint, scanning the ridge that lies ahead, the long valley of Scandale to the east and the knobbly hills that cluster around the northern edges of Windermere.

Retrace your steps to the main path, and, with one of Lakeland's splendid drystone walls for company, press on up ever-rising ground and rock steps to High Pike. Anyone expecting the rock to continue is in for a surprise for High Pike proves to be a sloping plateau of grass, possessing little rock save

Looking back over Low Pike to Windermere

that on which a small cairn has been perched.

Dove Crag lies ahead, at the end of a long, easily ascended grassy slope, up which the wall marches with determination. It is a determination, however, that expires within striking distance of the top of Dove Crag, there collapsing to a dilapidated shadow of its former self.

On first appearances there is nothing to detain you on Dove Crag (2), no crag, no doves, but if you continue north to a small and apparently insignificant cairn set amid a rash of stones, suddenly, a fantastic view opens up of Helvellyn, St Sunday Crag, Place Fell and the far eastern fells. But still there is no indication that below Dove Crag's ordinary dome lies one of Lakeland's most magnificent rock-climbing playgrounds, the great cliffs of the real Dove Crag.

As the route continues, escorted for a while longer by a now decidedly impoverished wall, so the going becomes distinctly more rocky. Tackling first the rocks of Hart Crag and then another rocky rise that has more shape about it than maps suggest, the path presses on westwards to the summit of Fairfield (3), a vast, rocky, featureless plateau that is inordinately disorientating in mist. Its height advantage seems to do little for Fairfield's worth as a viewpoint, but if you approach the northern and eastern edges of the summit plateau (with care, especially in winter when they are corniced) you will find yourself overlooking great ice-gouged corries and shapely

FACT FILE

Start/Finish Ambleside main car park,
GR 376046
Distance 16km (10 miles)
Height gain 970m (3180ft)
Walking time 6 hours
Type of walk A high mountain circuit, both long
and tiring. Good paths throughout, but the
summit of Fairfield is confusing in poor visibility.
In addition to an ice axe, crampons would be
useful in winter conditions

The Route in Brief

Start Leave Ambleside up Kirkstone Road and
Nook Lane to Low Sweden Bridge.
1 Follow rising path on to the main ridge and
ascend over Low Pike and High Pike to Dove
Crag, following a wall.
2 Continue across Hart Crag to Fairfield.
3 Descend (roughly W of S) to Great Rigg, and
continue along ridge, over Rydal Fell to Heron
Pike.
4 Continue descending, rockily, to Nab Scar,
dropping steeply to Rydal Mount.
5 Walk down to main road and turn L to
Ambleside.

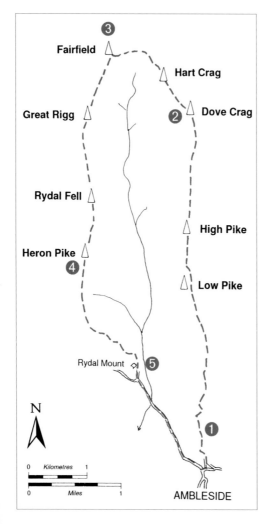

ridges and fells that do much to redeem
Fairfield's character.

Begin east of south down an increasing
slope that brings you first to Great Rigg,
before continuing in fine style over the bumps
of Rydal Fell and Heron Pike, all well trod-
den. Take care descending Great Rigg, where
shattered rocks lead down to a large cairn
marking the start of a branching ridge that
descends to Grasmere over Stone Arthur. This
is *not* the way to go; not today, anyway.

Momentum gathers as easy walking ensues
over Rydal Fell, directly above Erne Crag, and
on to the final summit, Heron Pike (**4**). As you
leave Heron Pike, so begins a long, rock-
bound, stony descent of Nab Scar, irksome in
ascent (which is why we are going this way
round), finally reaching the valley bottom not
far from Rydal Mount (**5**). Now is the time to
visit this sanctum of literary nostalgia, the
home of Wordsworth from 1813 to 1850. To
finish walk down to the main road and turn left
for an easy stroll back to Ambleside.

THE DEEPDALE HORSESHOE

This demanding day involves a complete high-level tour of Deepdale, a rather concealed valley tucked beneath the steepness of St Sunday Crag and the glacier-fashioned corries of Fairfield. Distance and height gain combine to suggest that this walk, one of the Lakeland classics, be left for a clear summer's day, when the conclusion close by a hotel will appeal to those who like their pub walks on the tough side.

Behind the Patterdale Hotel you will find a path leading through trees to a gate and on beside a wall, finally climbing to two adjacent gates. Take the left gate and continue by a wall (later a fence) to cross Hag Beck. Heading north-west cross more fields to reach the ridge below Thornhow End, at a gate and stile.

Turn left and climb steeply on a clear path to the top of Thornhow End, crossing the intake wall by a stile. Easier walking follows for a while but the obvious path avoids the minor top, Birks, to which you will have to

St Sunday Crag from Cofa Pike

Deepdale and Hartsop above How

divert, left, to climb the true line of the ridge. The highest point of Birks (1) is marked by a small cairn, from which the next stage, up on to St Sunday Crag, appears quite daunting, with the main line (rising on the right) and Gavel Pike (the east ridge of St Sunday Crag) forming a wide hollow, known as Gavel Moss. A path curves around the head of this hollow, and while this is easier than the main ridge line, it is less interesting and has limited views.

So, press on up the right hand ridge, reached across a grassy col from Birks, and climbing a rocky edge with fine views of Grisedale as compensation for the effort. A line of cairns guides you to the summit, a relaxed pile of rocks among rocks. To reach it be sure to leave the more prominent path, which for reasons that elude me has developed into a summit bypass – why put so much effort into getting here and then not visit the summit?

The long descent to Deepdale Hause is quite splendid and without difficulty, following a clear path. Grisedale lies down to your right, with Dollywaggon Pike, Grisedale Tarn and Seat Sandal forming an attractive arrangement, while to your left, the slopes of St Sunday Crag fall steeply into Deepdale. But as you descend your attention will be drawn to what awaits. A stony path races on to the great tumble of stones of Cofa Pike, across which a good path darts, before placing you at the foot of Fairfield. Along this section, the view of Fairfield's crags, particularly Hutaple Crag and the long descending ridge of your return, Hartsop above How, are outstanding and encourage you along.

The pull on to Fairfield is loose and stony and no doubt high on someone's list for 'improvement', but all the difficulties and exposure can be avoided with a little study, bringing you surprisingly quickly to the plateau-like top of the fell (2).

A line of cairns, initially south-east then east, lead off the fell top, placing you safely on the broad track to Hart Crag. On a clear day, a narrow path around the rim of Deepdale provides more exciting views, but this becomes corniced in winter conditions and should be avoided. Both paths combine above Link Cove and unseen Scrubby Crag, and take you down rockily across Link Hause and on towards Hart Crag (3). As you walk on, you can see the ridge of descent, steepish at first, before a long steady canter high above both Deepdale and Dovedale.

The start of the descending ridge as it leaves Hart Crag is moderately steep but not difficult. A little forethought as you tackle some easy-angled slabs, where there is a wee sense of exposure, will soon have you on easier grassy slopes, and the long crest of the ridge. A slight rise marks the highest point, just above Gill Crag, beyond which you meet a wall that accompanies you downward.

Keeping the wall always on your right, continue descending, cross an intermediate wall,

Start/Finish Car park, opposite Patterdale Hotel, GR 396159
Distance 14.5km (9 miles)
Height gain 995m (3265ft)
Walking time 6 hours
Type of walk A tough high mountain walk, mostly on good paths. Some loose rock on the ascent of Fairfield and a little exposure descending from Hart Crag

The Route in Brief

Start Locate and follow a signposted path at the rear of the Patterdale Hotel, and follow this, across Hag Beck to reach the base of Thornhow End. Climb L and divert from the path to reach the top of Birks.
1 Continue up right-hand ridge to top of St Sunday Crag and across the summit, pressing on, by a good path, over Cofa Pike, to climb steeply on to Fairfield.
2 Set off SE, E then SE again to reach Hart Crag.
3 Descend N of E, taking care on exposed slabs, to follow crest of Hartsop above How down to woodland. Fork L and continue down to main road at Deepdale Bridge. Follow road back to Patterdale.

and press on down steepening ground to enter woodland. When the path forks, go left to a stile over a wall, and follow a waymarked path (white arrows) through pastures to reach the main valley road at a gate, near Deepdale Bridge. Go left along the road, most of the tarmac bashing being avoidable, to return to Patterdale.

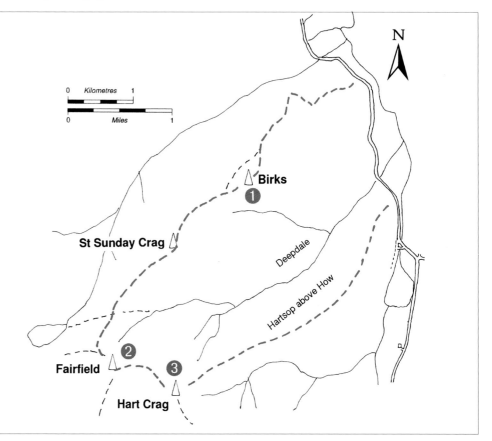

WANSFELL PIKE

Ambleside is a well-blessed centre for walkers. The tough and energetic have the magnificent Fairfield Horseshoe immediately to foot and more high summits not far distant, while those of a less adventurous nature may still enjoy the benefits of elevation by tackling Loughrigg Fell, or, as described here, Wansfell Pike. Unlike its companions, Wansfell Pike provides a grandstand view down the length of Windermere that alone makes a visit to this rather lowly summit eminently justified.

There are a number of car parks in Ambleside, though the main car park at the northern edge of the town is the most commodious. Leave it and turn right into the centre of town, and take the lane behind the Salutation Hotel (signposted: Waterfalls, Stockghyll and Wansfell Pike). Continue climbing above Stockghyll Park until you cross a cattle grid. On the way you can divert into the park to view the splendid falls, returning to the lane via a turnstile before reaching the cattle grid.

Not long after the cattle grid, climb a metal ladder and cross a stile to enter a field on the

Troutbeck village

right. A footpath pursues the course of a beck, climbing easily up the field to another ladder stile at the end of a walled track. Cross the track and go through a wall gap, still following the beck, as the path, renovated and waymarked in places, steeply continues its ascent, crossing the

beck before finally passing through a wall and scampering up to the summit (1). The summit, though not quite the highest point on this little ridge, commands a fine view in all directions and

a most dramatic prospect of Windermere.

The way now continues over the ridge to Troutbeck, setting off east across a fence and down a clear path to a gate, and on again to the walled Nanny Lane. Now turn right and follow Nanny Lane to reach the Troutbeck road (2) at Lane Foot Farm. Turn right and walk along the road to the post office. Just beyond the post office, leave the road for a track, Robin Lane (3) (signposted: Skelghyll, Jenkin Crag and Ambleside).

Robin Lane rises gently for a while and where it continues right as Hundred's Road, branch left through a gate for High Skelghyll, gradually descending to reach a metalled drive. Go right and follow it to High Skelghyll and continue past the farmhouse through gates. Along the stony track that follows you eventually enter Skelghyll Wood (4), and can shortly deviate to enjoy the celebrated view from Jenkin Crag.

Back on the woodland path, go right at a fork and zigzag down to a bridge over Stencher Beck. The main path (ignoring a branching path on the left) continues down and leaves the woodland to join an access lane merging into Old Lake Lane. Go right, to return to Ambleside town centre by a less busy route than the parallel A591, which it is eventually forced to join. Keep going through the town centre to return to the car park.

Left: Wansfell Pike

FACT FILE

Start/Finish Ambleside main car park, GR 376046
Distance 10km (6¼ miles)
Height gain 500m (1640ft)
Walking time 3½–4 hours
Type of walk A popular and straightforward walk

The Route in Brief
Start From the main car park go R into the town centre and follow the lane behind the Salutation Hotel until just after a cattle grid you cross a stile on the R and ascend fields to reach Wansfell Pike.

1 Continue E, descending to meet Nanny Lane and continue down this to Troutbeck village.

2 Turn R along road and after post office, branch R on to Robin Lane.

3 When Robin Lane forks, go L to pass High Skelghyll Farm and later enter Skelghyll Wood.

4 Keep on track through wood, and on leaving keep ahead to reach Old Lake Lane. Turn R to return to Ambleside town centre.

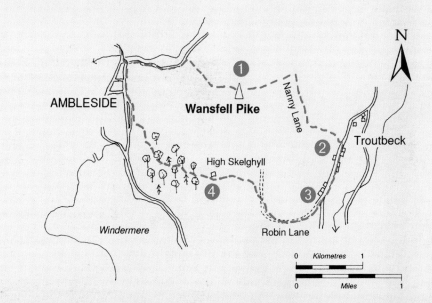

DOVE CRAG AND CAISTON BECK

Described by Jessica Lofthouse, that astute Lancastrian observer of nature in all its forms, as 'a sweet little dale, a green cradle among crags, sprinkled with hazel woods and berried rowans, with the beck, crystal-clear, chuckling over bright stones', Dovedale is a place you can instantly fall in love with. Indeed, one eighteenth-century writer described it as a soft and delicate maiden, though whether that would precipitate a *coup de foudre* these days is open to conjecture. Wild and rugged are also appropriate appellations to bestow on this sylvan dale for at its head rise the renowned precipices of Dove Crag on which routes were first pioneered as long ago as 1910.

This circuit is a journey through all that is best in Dovedale, and in returning down delightful Caiston Beck completes one of the most satisfying rounds in Lakeland.

From the Cow Bridge car park, set off over the nearby bridge over Goldrill Beck. Go instantly left through a gate on a broad track beside the beck and beneath wooded slopes of oak and beech that in springtime are alive with birdsong and bright with primroses, violets and wild garlic. Soon the beck opens out into the broad expanse of Brotherswater, once known as Broad Water, but renamed in memory of two brothers said to have drowned in its waters.

Beyond the end of the lake the path continues above alluvial pastures formed by debris long since washed down from the surrounding heights. At a gate, keep ahead to reach Hartsop Hall **(1)**. Hartsop Hall is a working farm, originally built in the sixteenth century and extensively altered since then. It was formerly the home of the de Lancaster family, and later of Sir John Lowther who became the first Viscount Lonsdale at the end of the seventeenth century.

At Hartsop Hall stay on a track going right to meet a signposted path heading left for Kirkstone Pass and Scandale. This is the way you will return at the end of the walk, but for now ignore it and keep right (signposted to Dove Crag) on a good path climbing steadily higher across the valley wall to a suspended cove beneath the fearsome cliffs of Dove Crag.

To the right of the crag locate a gully of scree and projecting rocks, quite frequently serving as a drain for the fellside above. Ascend this to reach Houndshope Cove, a high, wide hollow containing a small tarn, with Dove Crag on your left and Hart Crag and the long ridge of Hartsop above How on the right. Keep climbing to leave Houndshope Cove and you will find a line of cairns leading to a collapsed wall across the stony col between Hart Crag and Dove Crag. Turn left and follow the wall to the top of Dove Crag **(2)**.

The summit is unremarkable but the view it commands amply rewards the effort, being obstructed only to the north-west where the bulk of Fairfield sits Godfather-like at the head of its own family of mountains, its arms extended in a protective embrace around the valley of Rydal Beck.

The rest of the journey is almost all downhill and takes you into a corner of Lakeland only rarely visited. Set off by going south along the ridge, following the wall until you meet a fenceline shooting off at right angles. Turn along the fence (east) and keep to a path that descends grassy slopes. The going gets a little rougher before reaching the easier but often boggy stretch known as Bakestones Moss. Once again you get a fine view of the Dove Crag cliffs, high on which is a concealed cave,

Right: Dovedale and Dove Crag

84

known as the Priest Hole, probably quarried by dalesmen, but with a long history as a bivouac.

Beyond Bakestones Moss lies one of Lakeland's miniature gems, Little Hart Crag, a double-topped crag-girt fell in a splendid position at the head of Scandale. The surprising number of mini-crags are due to the remains of a stratum that geologists know as the Haweswater Syncline.

The path maintains faith with the fenceline as it bends sharply and runs down to Scandale Pass. To reach Little Hart Crag you must leave the path for a short while, for a little easy scrambling. Rejoin the path and complete the descent to Scandale Pass (3), there turning left to descend on a good path into beautiful Caiston Glen. Caiston Beck manages some attractive small waterfalls en route before it joins forces with Kirkstone Beck to flow into Brotherswater. As you descend Caiston Glen, the view ahead is largely dominated by Place Fell, while an ancient settlement near the apex of the confluence of Kirkstone Beck and Dovedale Beck is worth a quick inspection.

Cross Dovedale Beck and walk on through a clutch of gates to rejoin your outward route near Hartsop Hall.

Little Hart Crag and the head of Scandale

FACT FILE

Start/Finish Cow Bridge car park, Hartsop, GR 403134
Distance 12km (7½ miles)
Height gain 665m (2180ft)
Walking time 5 hours
Type of walk Fairly demanding and involving considerable ascent and descent. The steep grassy slopes above Bakestones Moss require care in winter conditions

The Route in Brief
Start Cross the bridge near the car park and turn L to follow a broad path through woodland. Continue as far as Hartsop Hall.
1 Bear R to follow a rising path into Dovedale and below Dove Crag climb a gully (on R) to reach the ridge-top wall. Turn L to the top of Dove Crag.

2 Follow wall S to meet fence and descend L with fence over Bakestones Moss, via Little Hart Crag, to head of Scandale Pass.
3 Descend L into Caiston Glen, and follow stream down to confluence with Dovedale Beck. Cross beck and walk on, towards Hartsop Hall. Retrace outward steps.

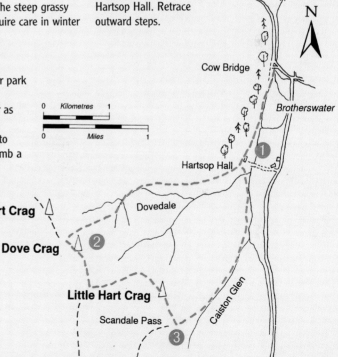

87

6

PATTERDALE

There is a tradition that the name Patterdale comes from St Patrick's Dale, after the Celtic St Patrick, one of three missionaries thought to have visited the region during the early fifth century, but historians are not unanimous. Others feel it derives from twelfth-century records in which the valley is called *Patrichesdale*, a combination of the Scandinavian word for valley and the Old Irish personal name, *Patraic*. Since there is no evidence of a Christian base in Patterdale before the end of the twelfth century, and most of the people who colonised the Lake District were Norsemen arriving from Ireland, it is feasible that the valley is named after an Irish-Norse farmer.

Whatever the derivation, Patterdale has long been a popular valley in spite of having at one end a high mountain pass that in winter is often a barrier to anyone approaching from Troutbeck, Ambleside and Windermere. The so-called Lake Poets greatly loved the place, and its attractions brought not only the Wordsworths, but Sir Walter Scott, Sir Humphrey Davy the English scientist, and others. It was at Gowbarrow Park that Dorothy Wordsworth noticed the daffodils that led to her brother William penning what is perhaps his best-remembered poem, *I Wandered Lonely as a Cloud*.

It is from Wordsworth's *Guide to the Lakes* (5th edition, 1835) that something is learned of the history of Brotherswater, that attractive lake set near the confluence of Hartsop and Dovedale:

As we descend, Patterdale opens upon the eye in grand simplicity, screened by mountains, and proceeding from two heads, Deepdale and Hartshope (sic), where lies the little lake of Brothers-water, named in old maps Broaderwater, and probably rightly so...but the change in appellation of this small lake or pool (if it be a corruption) may have been assisted by some melancholy accident similar to what happened about twenty years ago, when two brothers were drowned there, having gone out to take their holiday pleasure upon the ice on a new-year's day.

There is something truly inspiring about Patterdale. As you descend from the Kirk Stone so the road ahead unwinds, side streams begin to fashion miniature waterfalls to brighten the landscape, and then a series of delectable

Right: Patterdale from the walk up to Boardale Hause
Opposite: Looking down on Grisedale

glens feed into the main valley, Caiston Glen, Dovedale, Hartsop, through which flows Hayeswater Beck, Deepdale, Grisedale, Glenridding, Glencoynedale. Each of these glens invites exploration, possible only on foot, while as you reach Patterdale itself you become aware of well-established pathways rising across the fells to the east. They pass into yet another world, a more intimate version of Patterdale, a region of smaller valleys collectively known as Martindale.

But it is the lake which commands attention. Its distinctive, curving form revealing new vistas at every bend supports the view that Ullswater is one of the most outstandingly beautiful stretches of water in the Lake District. Celia Fiennes, a noted early traveller throughout Britain, on her *Great Journey to Newcastle and to Cornwall* in 1698, commented on it:

Lake Steamer, Ullswater

> '...*it's full of such sort of stones and slatts in the bottom as the other* [Windermere], *neer the brimm where its shallowe you see it cleer to the bottom; this is secured on each side by such formidable heights as those rocky fells in the same manner as the other was.*'

A survey today of the visitors to Patterdale will reveal a wide range of purpose. Many come to tackle Striding Edge and the high summits of the Helvellyn and Fairfield massifs, others to amble more leisurely around the lake shores, or to indulge in the delightful walk to Silver Bay; yet more are intent on aquatic pursuit. They all come to Patterdale: ramblers, fell walkers, cyclists, motor cyclists, caravanners, campers, yachting people, anglers, rock climbers, day trippers, holiday-makers – and Patterdale consumes them all. Everyone, as were the Wordsworths, is enchanted by the valley and its supreme *à la carte* menu of recreational enjoyment. It is much loved, and always will be.

THE GRISEDALE HORSESHOE

This circuit of Grisedale gives a long and demanding mountain day, one sure to please those robust enough to take it on. On the work hard, play hard scale, this horseshoe scores a full ten. The ascent begins steeply in order to achieve Birkhouse Moor, and then goes on to tackle Striding Edge. From Helvellyn a much easier stretch brings you down to visit Grisedale Tarn, before the steady grind up on to Fairfield. A rugged, splendid descent over Cofa Pike and on to St Sunday Crag presages the final stages, over Birks, and so down to Patterdale for a brief road-bashing conclusion.

Leave the main car park in Glenridding and walk back to the road, turning right to cross Glenridding Bridge, and immediately right on to a narrow road past the post office and the public hall. The road degenerates to a track and forks a short way on. Take the signposted route to Lanty's Tarn and Striding Edge, a variable commodity at times as erosion control work deflects the original route. Eventually, you arrive at Lanty's Tarn, an idyllic setting embraced by trees that do much to enhance the scene. The tarn used to be natural, but was dammed to serve the needs of Patterdale Hall. If you look beyond the trees, you see the dark form of St Sunday Crag and Birks looming in the distance. It may seem incredible now, but that is where you are going, by a roundabout route.

Before the end of the tarn is reached a path ascends right, following a wall. Take this and cross the wall at a gate. Now follow a path that uses the wall as a guide to the top of Birkhouse Moor, quite a steep proposition. At the top, where the wall bends left, a cairn, off to the right, marks what many regard as the top of Birkhouse Moor, but its bumpy nature confounds precision. If you turn left along the wall, you will cross another raised section, which large scale maps reveal as the true, but far less appealing, summit (1).

As you stroll beside the wall, Helvellyn lies directly ahead, Striding Edge to its left, and the shapely cone of Catstyecam on the right. The wall changes direction near its junction with the more conventional route from Grisedale, at the Hole in the Wall. Between this point and the top of Helvellyn lie four distinct sections. The first is an easy, ever-so-gently rising path bringing Red Tarn into view and gradually approaching the real rock work.

Then, from a narrow col, you scramble around the highest point along the ridge, High Spying How, never quite crossing the crest, unless you make a point of doing so, which many do. Immediately before the next section, through a narrow gap and round a rocky corner stands the Dixon Memorial, commemorating a houndsman who fell to his death from the ridge in 1858.

A slight descent is needed before crossing to the third section, which begins with flat ledges on the very top of the ridge. The way soon moves down to the right, abandoning the crest for psychologically easier going just below it. Purists will stick to the crest throughout, but should **not** be so foolhardy as to do so in windy conditions. At the end of this section, the *pièce de résistance* comes in the form of a neat rock gully, most easily negotiated, I find, by climbing down backwards. There are a multitude of hand- and footholds, but people of a nervous disposition may well find cause to doubt me! Finally – don't relax your concentration yet – two distinct scrambly bumps lead to a steep slope of loose rock and stones before pulling on to the grassy edge of the Helvellyn plateau.

There is nothing fit walkers cannot tackle along Striding Edge, in normal conditions. All

Helvellyn from the Hole in the Wall

of the difficulties, such as they are, can be bypassed, initially on the right and then, circumventing that final gully, on the left. In winter it is a different thing altogether, with little, if any, margin for error.

As you reach the top, you are ushered right on a broad path, past the Gough Memorial, to a four-berth shelter, and then up a little rise, the highest point, to a barren, flat summit **(2)** on which stands a forlorn trig pillar. The view, unhindered by adjoining peaks, is as far reaching as air conditions will allow.

The Gough Memorial, perched directly above Red Tarn, commemorates Charles Gough, who fell to his death in 1805. For three months his dog kept vigil over its master's body, a tale that inspired the quills of both William Wordsworth and Walter Scott.

From Helvellyn you shoot off southwards to Dollywaggon Pike, on a blazed trail so pronounced you can follow it on the most Stygian night; yet it is needlessly marked by a multitude of cairns, swept into neat little piles like autumn leaves ready for disposal. In the dark, you see the path and stumble over the cairns. A more adventurous line simply follows the rim above Nethermost Cove and Ruthwaite Cove, a far less pedestrian way of continuing the walk, overlooking a craggy, ice-gouged landscape.

From Dollywaggon Pike's lofty summit above Cock Cove, you speed down steeply to a welcome break on the shores of Grisedale Tarn **(3)**, and decision time. From here the walk ascends Fairfield and then continues over St Sunday Crag. If you are bursting with energy you can go round the tarn and take in Seat Sandal, in that way sticking faithfully to the Grisedale watershed. If, on the other hand, you are tired, you can omit Fairfield by using a slanting path rising north of east from near the outflow of the tarn, to Deepdale Hause. If you are feeling very tired, forego these extra heights and go down the well-trodden path into Grisedale.

A good path runs around the south side of Grisedale Tarn to Grisedale Hause, from where a steep, rocky grind leads eastwards by a dilapidated wall to the top of Fairfield. When the wall ends, a line of cairns, this time useful, lead on to the potentially confusing summit.

Leave it by going north and descending a rocky stairway to cross Cofa Pike, a shapely pile, beyond which a broad track presses on to Deepdale Hause, and then rises in great steps to the top of St Sunday Crag **(4)**.

A long descent now follows, along a cairned path to the top of a rocky ridge that continues more steeply to a grassy col, near Birks. Ignore a prominent path crossing the fell slopes of Birks and cross instead the top of this outlier and go on down more grassy slopes to rejoin the main path above Thornhow End, at a stile. Keep descending to reach the road that serves Grisedale, and turn right downhill to the A592, the main valley road. Turn left and take a path beside the road on the left for the brief conclusion to Glenridding.

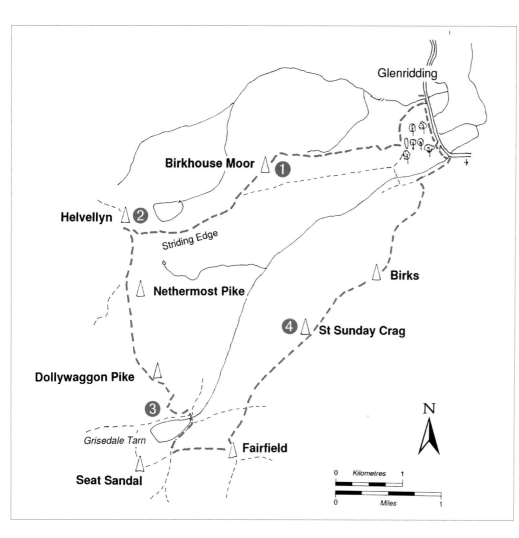

Glenridding

Birkhouse Moor △ ❶

Helvellyn △ ❷

Striding Edge

△ Nethermost Pike

△ Birks

❹ △ St Sunday Crag

Dollywaggon Pike △

❸

Grisedale Tarn

Fairfield △

Seat Sandal △

N

| 0 | Kilometres | 1 |
| 0 | Miles | 1 |

Start/Finish Glenridding car park, GR 386169
Distance 17.5km (10³/₄ miles)
Height gain 1440m (4725ft)
Walking time 8–8¹/₂ hours
Type of walk A long and demanding high mountain walk, suitable only for a clear day and strong, experienced walkers. Probably too long an undertaking for winter conditions

The Route in Brief

Start Leave the car park and return to the main road. Turn R and immediately R, to follow path to Lanty's Tarn. Go R beside a wall to reach the top of Birkhouse Moor.
1 Continue alongside wall to Hole in Wall and cross Striding Edge to gain the summit of Helvellyn.
2 Continue over Nethermost Pike and Dollywaggon Pike to Grisedale Tarn.
3 Ascend Fairfield from Grisedale Hause and descend N to reach Cofa Pike, continuing on to St Sunday Crag.
4 Descend over Birks to reach minor road and turn R to main valley road. Turn L to Glenridding.

AIRA FORCE AND GOWBARROW FELL

Gathering its waters far in the grassy folds of Deepdale, Aira Force is one of Lakeland's most endearing waterfalls. The land around was purchased by the National Trust in 1913 and has been landscaped as a Victorian park. The fall, though of unspectacular height, brings light to Molly Lefebure's '...chasm of green tree-filled gloom', and is a delightful place to visit at any time of year. Here it is combined with a wide, sweeping tour of Gowbarrow Fell, formerly a medieval deer park, and retaining stretches of bleak, rock-punctuated moorland dotted with gnarled oak trees. Gowbarrow, inevitably, is ever associated with Wordsworth's daffodils, noticed and recorded by his sister Dorothy in her journal in 1802, but the hinterland above and beyond provides a welcome respite from more heavily populated walking areas.

Leave the Aira Force car park by a gate at its northern end and follow a path to another gate. Go right and descend through woodland to a footbridge spanning Aira Beck,

Aira Force

here flowing through a deep ravine. Cross the bridge and climb a flight of steps on the opposite bank, where the path divides. Take the lower path, in places close to a steep drop to the beck, and eventually reach a stone bridge near the foot of Aira Force.

Over the bridge you climb more steps to join another path, bearing right to cross a higher bridge. Now back on the true left bank of the stream, follow the path above the falls, ignoring any pathways branching off to higher levels.

The whole area around Aira Force is very attractive, and even the two stone bridges you encounter have been constructed in differing styles. The lower is made of vertical stones, not traditional in these parts, while the higher has horizontal stones, more in keeping with the dale customs.

Staying on the continuing path through oak woodland you arrive at a higher waterfall, High Force. Look for a gate and a sign indicating a footpath to Dockray and Ulcat Row. Follow this through thinning woodland, passing a wall before reaching open bracken heath and a faint track above a wall (signposted to Ulcat Row). The path shepherds you on through another gate, and changes direction as it negotiates Norman Crag (1) at the north-western edge of Gowbarrow Fell. Now it heads north-east to meet a quiet country lane at a gate, not far from Ulcat Row.

The stretch of road walking that now ensues is extremely pleasant and virtually traffic free; it is justified by the opportunity it creates to return through Swinburn's Park. Turn right along the road, continuing to a T-junction (2), where you turn right to begin a short uphill section to reach The Hause (3), a neat col beneath the slopes of Little Mell Fell.

Go down the road, ignore the turning to Dacre, and as you descend so you see an escarpment develop on the right. This is Priest's Crag and the continuing route lies across its base, reached by a gate at the side of the road. The path beyond rises gradually to a col near Gate Crags, directly above Hagg Wood, and continues rising, through another gate and on below Little Meldrum. In places the path is muddy as it contours round Great Meldrum and Kirksty Brow until, at a wall, you re-enter National Trust property, near the ruins of a shooting lodge (4).

Heading south, climb slightly to cross three streams all feeding into Collierhagg Beck and Ullswater. When the path divides, take the left branch, dropping a little before climbing once again and swinging right, around a corner with the top of Yew Crag, a popular viewpoint, in sight below and to your left.

Follow the ongoing path, heading down to a path junction near Lyulph's Tower, an eighteenth-century folly constructed by one of the dukes of Norfolk. It stands on or near the site of the fortress of Lyulph, the first Baron Greystoke. Lyulph stems from *ulf*, or *l'ulf*, Scandinavian for wolf, and leads into Ulf's Water, or Ullswater.

After the tower ignore a gate on your left and bear right to another gate, beyond, keep left to a stile in a fence corner. Soon after this you rejoin the Aira Force path, to retrace your steps to the car park.

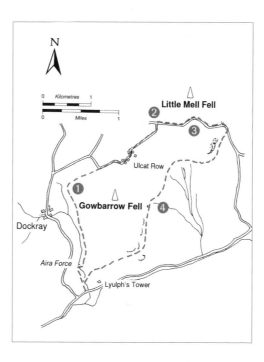

FACT FILE

Start/Finish Aira Force car park, GR 401201
Distance 13km (8 miles)
Height gain 395m (1295ft)
Walking time 4–4½ hours
Type of walk Some steep walking beside Aira Force, but otherwise moderate

The Route in Brief
Start Leave the car park at its northern end and follow pathways across Aira Beck and below Aira Force, finally to emerge above the falls, heading N with the beck, before moving away to round Norman Crag.
1 Continue to meet road near Ulcat Row and follow this to a T-junction.
2 Go R to reach The Hause.
3 Descend, ignoring L turn to Dacre, to reach gate on R. Pass below Priest's Crag and follow path into Swinburn's Park, re-entering NT property near a shooting lodge.
4 Follow path S to Yew Crag, and then W to path junction above Lyulph's Tower. Beyond, the path goes through gates/stile to rejoin Aira Force path.

95

THE HARTSOP ROUND

The summits to the east of the Kirkstone Pass are hardly unfamiliar to visitors who use this high, and in winter sometimes dangerous mountain pass. Yet, in any survey of most frequently visited Lakeland fells, it will be some time before anyone mentions the vast area of mountain upland delineated by the Patterdale valley and Kirkstone on the west, and the A6 at Shap in the east. This is a wild, lonely and amorphous area, where moorland stretches contrast with the beauty of verdant valleys; a soft, rounded hinterland with few savage intrusions; an area of harmonious companions. At its heart rises High Street, made eternally famous by Roman navvies, who built a road across its spacious summit, linking their forts at Galava, near Ambleside and Brocavum (Brougham), at the confluence of the Lowther and Eamont rivers. To visit these heights from Patterdale valley is an invigorating outing, superb in winter, if you are fully and properly equipped (crampons will be needed), and breathtaking in summer.

Left: Summit cairn on Thornthwaite Crag
Opposite: Barn in Hartsop

From the car park set off along the main road heading towards Hartsop. There is a car park on the fell side of Hartsop village, but an approach along the road from Cow Bridge, turning left along the minor road for Hartsop, allows you to warm up gently and introduces you to the delights of this sheltered village, lying as it does in a side valley, off the main Patterdale valley.

Hartsop retains many features that tell of its former self-sufficiency as a mountain community – a corn-drying kiln, spinning galleries and traces of lead mining near the confluence of Pasture Beck and Hayeswater Gill. Spinning galleries are a familiar characteristic of Lakeland farm architecture, formed by carrying the roof beyond the wall, the space beneath the extended eaves providing useful storage space.

Beyond the village the second car park (1) is encountered. Leave it by a gate and turn right, immediately to cross the nearby gill by a bridge. Turn left on to a good path running beside a wall. It soon swings right into Threshthwaite (pronounced *Thresh'et*) Glen, following the line of Pasture Beck. The walk into this side glen, less favoured than most, is delightful, and ascends gradually into an upper glen, Threshthwaite Cove, beneath the cliffs of Raven Crag. Progressively the valley closes in and a short steep pull leads to Threshthwaite Mouth **(2)**, with the long, beautiful valley of Troutbeck stretching out ahead.

A wall crossing Threshthwaite Mouth provides shelter from any winds breezing across the col, and ascends all the way to Thornthwaite Crag **(3)**: should cloud settle in, this is a safe and reliable guide. The section from the col requires considerable attention, and not a little effort, but in it lies the key to a long, rewarding and lofty traverse. This energetic section is never as long as it seems and as you ascend the view improves with every step, westward across Stony Cove Pike to Red Screes and the high central mountains of lakeland. To say that the highest point of Thornthwaite Crag is marked by a cairn is a classic understatement; no one is ever likely to forget the towering monolith standing in an angle in the wall.

From Thornthwaite Crag cross the wall and set off on the line of a good path that starts off south of east and then curves northeastwards to join the Roman road. The ancient road does not cross the summit of High Street **(4)**, and the simplest way of ensuring you find the trig marking the summit of this enormous whaleback is to leave the road after about fifteen minutes and move obliquely right to the wall which traverses the summit. This will lead you unerringly to the top.

High Street has long been a centre of

Start/Finish Small car park near Cow Bridge alongside the A592, GR 403134
Distance 12km (7½ miles)
Height gain 655m (2150ft)
Walking time 5–6 hours
Type of walk Energetic mountain walk through outstanding terrain

The Route in Brief

Start Walk along the road towards Hartsop village, turning into its access road and walking through the village to a car park.
1 Leave the car park and turn R heading for a bridge spanning a stream. Continue along the line of Pasture Beck and climb to Threshthwaite Mouth.
2 Follow wall steeply to Thornthwaite Beacon.
3 Cross wall and follow curving path towards High Street, leaving the path on reaching a wall and following that to the summit.
4 Continue along broad plateau-like summit, to cross Straits of Riggindale and circle round The Knott.
5 Descend steeply to outflow of Hayeswater and follow broad, descending track back to Hartsop.

attraction. In 1955, Sir Clement Jones, youngest son of the vicar of Burneside, mentions High Street, 'on whose flat top horse-racing and wrestling and athletic sports and all sorts of fun used to be enjoyed'. Even today, on some maps, the summit is called 'Racecourse Hill'.

Beyond High Street's summit plateau the ridge narrows abruptly to the Straits of Riggindale, with a grand view down the valley of that name to the far eastern fells of Lakeland. And as you cross the Straits, follow the wall on your left, avoiding a path diverging right to Rampsgill Head, and in only a few minutes you reach The Knott **(5)**, a fine, slightly conical hill. The path does not divert to this minor summit (though you can), but continues instead around it to a wall, and a long, easy descent of grassy slopes, to the outflow of Hayeswater. From Hayeswater dam, it is a simple, descending stroll on a broad path back to Hartsop.

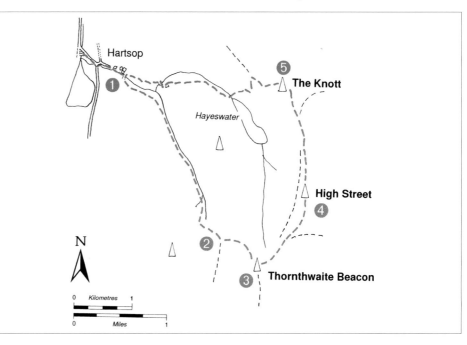

PLACE FELL

This inspection of Place Fell although brief nevertheless involves considerable height gain, steep at times both going up and coming down. The effort is rewarded with stunning views and a fell circuit that is one of the most beautiful in the Lake District. In summer you can enhance the experience by sailing across to Howtown from Glenridding, but do check the times of the ferries before committing yourself.

Beside the minor road into Sandwick, a signpost points out the way to Patterdale, along a cart track, beside a wall. Follow this as far as the footbridge over Scalehow Beck **(1)**, and keep on a short distance further to its highest point, near a wall corner, from where you can escape the track by taking to a path ascending the fellside. Scalehow Force can be seen through trees on the left and makes a memorable sight after prolonged rain.

The path climbs steeply, trending left to reach a shoulder, beyond which it zigzags upwards, finally pulling up to the large cairn that marks the top of Low Birk Fell **(2)**.

The continuing line on to Birk Fell, the north-western shoulder of Place Fell, is a combination of ever rising brackeny pathways, humps and hollows and craggy protuberances, finally reaching Bleaberry Knott, the heathery top of Birk Fell, where in late summer daily rations can be supplemented by a feast of bilberries.

Ahead rises The Knight, a towering lump, with the top of Place Fell beyond. Cross a stretch of boggy ground and more knolls and hollows, to meet a clear path rising from the direction of Ullswater. Take this, and at a col, go left along the rocky ridge that leads to The Knight.

To reach the top of Place Fell **(3)**, retreat to the col and tackle another small ridge that leads to the summit. The trig point commands an outstanding position atop a small rocky upthrust, and is a most tranquil place early in the morning or in the late afternoon.

From the summit head north-east, on a good path along the ridge of Hart Crag, passing a small tarn on the way. This brings you to a col, at Low Moss, beyond which the path forks. Go right and up on to High Dodd, bearing left to reach the summit **(4)**.

Now go right, descending grassy slopes; avoid a more direct route, which is craggy and confusing. Dropping through bracken you soon rejoin the main path and you should

Ullswater and Place Fell

follow this until it bears right to descend steeply above Boardale. Do not continue downwards, however, but bear left on to Sleet Fell.

From Sleet Fell, follow a collapsed wall down the western side of the fell, which lower down vanishes into bracken, but swings round to meet a path arriving from Low Moss, which will steer you down either to the road, or to the signpost near Sandwick at which the walk began.

Above: Place Fell from Boardale Hause
Left: Place Fell

FACT FILE

Start/Finish Sandwick, GR 423196. Limited parking – consider using ferry service from Glenridding
Distance 8km (5 miles)
Height gain 745m (2445ft)
Walking time 3–4 hours
Type of walk Rough in places, with steep ascents and descents. Confusing in mist

The Route in Brief

Start Leave Sandwick on the track to Patterdale, as far as Scalehow Beck.
1 Cross the footbridge and continue to the high point of the path, then leave it to ascend the fellside, negotiating rocky shoulders to reach Low Birk Fell.
2 Continue through more hummocky terrain, rising all the time, over Birk Fell (Bleaberry Knott) and The Knight, to reach the top of Place Fell.
3 Descend NE, down the line of Hart Crag to Low Moss (escape L if needed), and High Dodd.
4 Descend grassy eastern side of High Dodd, to continue along main path until it starts descending towards Boardale, but bear L to reach Sleet Fell, and from there follow dilapidated wall down to lower path, and return to Sandwick.

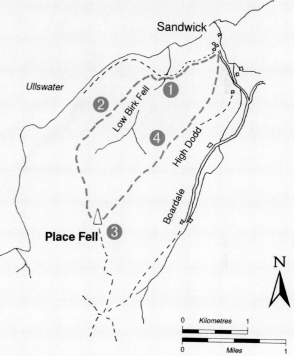

ANGLETARN PIKES AND HAYESWATER

This delightful visit to Angletarn Pikes and the accompanying tarn is one of the most pleasurable walks from Patterdale, and, with only modest effort, within the capacity of everyone. Here, the walk is extended to visit Hayeswater, beneath the slopes of High Street and Gray Crag, returning through the village of Hartsop, described by Molly Lefebure in *Cumbrian Discovery* as 'quaint in the truest sense of that much abused word'.

Leave the car park opposite the Patterdale Hotel and turn right, walking down the road as far as the George Starkey Memorial Hut. Leave the road here and follow a broad track leading to Side Farm, crossing Goldrill Beck on the way. It is a constrained stream now, but following the last Ice Age was responsible for depositing much of the alluvium that forms the flat spread of the dale at this point.

Go between the buildings at Side Farm (1) and turn right to follow a broad track towards the houses and cottages at Rooking. At a gate, turn left, to pass through another gate, and in so doing reach the imposing open flanks of Place Fell. Follow a path, up and right, with the way to Boardale Hause running ahead of you. At a fork, take to the higher path to arrive at a bench with an outstanding view.

The ongoing path now plods uneventfully upwards to Boardale Hause (2), a flat, grassy col between hillocks, and from which a number of pathways radiate. A few foundations on the hause are supposed to be those of a thirteenth-century church, though it would have been incredibly small. Boardale Hause was once a popular route to Penrith and a church here would be logical, serving both Patterdale and Martindale beyond.

On reaching Boardale Hause you soon see a couple of collapsed cairns, near which you should move right, to cross a small beck, ignoring all the paths going off to the left. Across the beck, the path is never in doubt as it negotiates a procession of twists and turns, ups and downs and grassy knolls until, just as Angletarn Pikes first ease into view, there is a stunning view down to Brotherswater and up the doodled line of the Kirkstone Pass.

The path presses on easily, until, with a final flourish you can leave it near the foot of the Pikes and ascend to the northernmost (and highest) top, from there crossing a brief boggy hollow to reach the southern top and its view of Angle Tarn (3) reposing in a broad mountain basin below. The tarn is a curvaceous patch of water dotted with tiny islands in a most tranquil setting, making this a suitable spot for a break.

Head down towards the tarn to rejoin the main path, left earlier, and follow it round Angle Tarn, climbing easily, with improving views, to a more level section approaching Satura Crag. Go through a gate, keeping below Satura Crag, and a short way on cross a boggy stretch as you deal with Prison Gill and Sulphury Gill.

Ahead the great grass-flanked hollow that contains Hayeswater, rises to a superb ring of fells, Gray Crag on the right, across Thornthwaite Crag to High Street, the Straits of Rigindale, and the nearby summit of The Knott. On a clear day, extending this walk to visit The Knott is unlikely to call for excess effort, and adds another fell summit to the day.

Once across Sulphury Gill you meet a path ascending from Hayeswater and this should be followed down to the outflow (4), from where a broad track leads right, out of the valley. Keep on, through the car park at the

Angle Tarn and Angletarn Pikes

Start/Finish Car park opposite Patterdale Hotel, GR 396159
Distance 12.5km (7³/₄ miles)
Height gain 430m (1410ft)
Walking time 4–5 hours
Type of walk Moderate effort, on good paths, with little ascent once Angletarn Pikes are reached

The Route in Brief

Start Leave the car park and go R, along the main road as far as the George Starkey Memorial Hut, and turn R to Side Farm.
1 Turn R on track to gate and L through another gate on to open fell. Climb R, ascending to Boardale Hause.
2 Cross stream and follow good path through undulating terrain to ascend to Angletarn Pikes, and then descend to Angle Tarn.
3 Continue below Satura Crag and across two gills to meet path rising from Hayeswater. Descend to Hayeswater.
4 Go R and down to Hartsop, continuing almost to main road. Turn R on back road, as far as Rooking, and there turn L along lane, back to Patterdale.

approach to Hartsop, and on through the village until, just before reaching the main valley road (A592), you can turn right on a minor access road (degenerating to a track). This takes a pleasant line along the base of the fells, past Dubhow, Beckstones and Crookabeck, until, on reaching Rooking, you take a minor road, left, back to Patterdale and the car park.

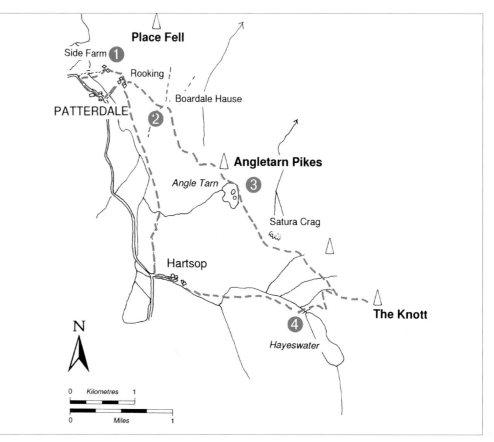

BOARDALE AND ULLSWATER

Embracing one of the finest low-level walks in Lakeland and a visit to a quiet, isolated valley, this circular walk is delightful. A modest amount of pastoral lane walking is the price you pay for outstanding scenery and the near certainty, out of season, that much of the time will be spent in the only form of solitary confinement that might be regarded as highly prized.

Set off from the car park, opposite the Patterdale Hotel and go left into the village, to a bend, where you take a minor road leading, left, over Goldrill Bridge, to the group of cottages at Rooking. Follow the road up to a gate and turn right, through it, to gain the foot slopes of Place Fell, and follow a path, slanting right, across the fellside to Boardale Hause (**1**). On some maps Boardale, the valley of the wild boars, is spelt Boredale, and various books on the subject offer both renditions. 'Boardale', and its natural history connotation, is rather more apposite, and so preferred here.

As you reach Boardale Hause, go left on a gently rising path that soon forks. Take the right branch, keeping ahead to reach a dramatic viewpoint at the head of an unsuspected rocky gully, at the head of Boardale. Descend the gully with care – the upper section is loose but soon becomes a more stable path easing down into the valley. The impression of walking into the landscape is very real; the valley before you, bounded on the left by Place Fell and on the right by Beda Fell, is stunning, leading the eye to distant Hallin Fell.

The path leads unerringly down to Boardalehead Farm (**2**), where you meet the valley road. Normally, you can keep ahead, through the farm, but if it is busy, please use a permissive path that goes around the farm, on the left. The road then leads on in the company of Boardale Beck, and later crosses it at a good spot for a breather.

Stay with the road until you can take a branching road to the left leading down to Sandwick. Ignore another road (on the right) as you approach Doe Green Farm, and keep on around the grassy spur of Sleet Fell as far as a signpost on the left (**3**), pointing out the way back to Patterdale. Go left here, abandoning the road, and take to a good path, near a wall.

Along the lake shore path

105

Beyond the footbridge of Scalehow Beck, the path heads for the Ullswater shoreline, of which there have been inviting glimpses all along the path. Between Scalehow Beck and Silver Bay, the walking is superb, following a jinking pathway that, for once happily, seems to go on forever. Just after a stretch of woodland walking, Silver Bay is reached, another perfect spot for a rest, but one you will find difficult to leave.

As you continue round Silver Point, so the path, having twisted and turned, now opts for undulating progress as a series of dips and cols draws you along the lake to its end. Here the path widens into a farm track and descends towards Side Farm (4). At the farm, turn right, between buildings, and follow the access road out to the main valley road, reaching it at the George Starkey Memorial Hut. Turn left, to reach the car park in a few minutes.

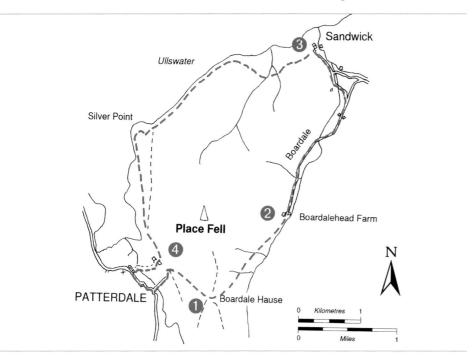

Start/Finish Car park opposite Patterdale Hotel, GR 396159
Distance 13km (8 miles)
Height gain 300m (985ft)
Walking time 4–5 hours
Type of walk Moderate difficulty, most of the uphill effort is in the ascent to Boardale Hause. The shore path and its many undulations can prove tiring

The Route in Brief
Start Leave the car park and go L to a road bend, and there L again down lane to Rooking. Through gate, and follow slanting path, R, to Boardale Hause.
1 Keep ahead across Hause, to reach top of Boardale, and descend to Boardalehead Farm.
2 Follow valley road to signpost near Sandwick.
3 Go L on path beside wall and follow clear pathway beside Ullswater, via Silver Bay, to Side Farm.
4 Go R, between farm buildings and take farm access out to valley road. Turn L to car park.

Left: Looking down on Boardale

7

MARDALE, KENTMERE AND LONGSLEDDALE

The instant beauty of Lakeland is readily found for it is all around you, embracing you, gazing down on you, awaiting you at every turn in the road. It is, superficially, satisfying; you come away having enjoyed a day, a week, or more, in a beautiful region of Britain. But the deeper beauty, the 'inner-person', the 'real' Lakeland, needs to be discovered, for it does not sit there blatantly advertising its attractions. Instead, you must come, visit, return, explore and wait; through all the weathers, in all the seasons. Then, when you are least expecting it, the charm of the Lakes will unfold.

A hint of what you are looking for lies in three valleys running along the south-eastern side of the region – Mardale, Kentmere and Longsleddale. Ironically, these are the nearest dales to the vast majority of visitors reaching the Lake District, yet they are hurried by, often unsuspected.

Submerged to satisfy the needs of distant conurbations for water, the valley of Mardale is slowly adjusting to man's intrusion, nature is having her way and the signs of man's endeavour are becoming less evident with each passing

Autumnal colours at Burbanks

year. Some of the original Mardale can be seen around the head of the valley, in the side dales, and at times when drought lays bare the skeleton framework of the drowned hamlet. Then it is not a happy sight, but when the sun shines brightly and the lake is full you can imagine a less contrived landscape, almost as if nature is making the best of a bad job.

To the south, Kentmere shares with Mardale some of the most noble scenery, rising to the broad back of High Street, used by Romans as a route between their forts at Ambleside and Brougham. South of the village of Kentmere lies what remains of a lake, its former self diminished to extend the acres of pastureland. The village's sixteenth-century church commemorates St Cuthbert, who was brought this way in his coffin bound for burial at Durham. In its grounds you will find a yew that has stood for five centuries, and nearby at the foot of the Garburn Pass into Troutbeck, twelve generations of the Gilpin family once lived, at Kentmere Hall. From this quiet retreat they grew to become preachers, writers, doctors and artists.

Mardale and Kentmere, of the three dales with which this section is concerned, are quite well known, but Longsleddale invariably features very, very late in anyone's exploration of the Lake District. Like its brethren, and many more about, it is a blind valley. Unlike its neighbours it does not have a lake, man-made or otherwise. But perhaps this is a God-send, protecting it from the inevitable through route and the consequences that brings.

Here in this delectable corner of the Lakes you will find another Wasdale, another Borrowdale and another of the numerous Mosedales that litter the map of the region. Here, too, you experience a quiet charm that typifies these fringe dales, a quality that would be destroyed if the valleys were ringed with high summits or vertiginous crags, a quality that balances the weight of Lakeland's attractions.

High Street and the long line of fells that flow north and south from it are a barrier to the east, yet they are of that ilk – rounded moorland fells, swathed in grass through which rocks thrust in an uncomfortable, tentative fashion. For the walker this vast, straggling area is a wonderland. Often you need good navigational skills, and always the willingness to cope with solitude and unending peace.

THE HAWESWATER SHORE PATH

Although long stretches of this circular walk have been in use for some time – the north shore route is part of the Northern Coast to Coast Walk – only during 1995 was a complete link made possible in a partnership between the National Park authority and North West Water. The path is dedicated to the memory of Bill Foster, Director of Conservation for North West Water, who died in November 1994. The route goes through Naddle Forest, a Site of Special Scientific Interest, where the red squirrel still survives; and passes land managed by the Royal Society for the Protection of Birds, home to many rare species, including the golden eagle.

To avoid congesting the limited parking area at Mardale, the walk begins at Burnbanks and goes anti-clockwise, to gain the best of available sunlight.

Start by going up a narrow path beside the telephone box to reach a roughly surfaced lane. Go left, past cottages that once housed men working on the reservoir and dam, and soon reach woodland. Follow the broad trail right and left to a gate in a boundary fence.

Beyond the gate the track continues across the base of open, craggy slopes clad in bracken, and dotted with hawthorn, rowan and gorse. The track climbs gently to a level section, where the reservoir, glimpsed through trees, comes into view along with (ahead on the right) the hanging valley of Fordingdale, through which flows Measand Beck.

A stone tablet placed in the wall announces that the waters of Heltondale Beck and Hows Beck were diverted into the reservoir in October 1959. A similar tablet on the opposite side accounts for the demise of Naddle Beck and Swindale Beck, which suffered the same fate two years earlier, almost to the day.

The track continues uneventfully, accompanied either by a wall or a fence, and rising on the right to a conspicuous cairn on Four Stones Hill. A stretch of clear ground on the left allows a fine view up the length of Haweswater to the ring of summits at its head.

Near the ruins of a homestead, the broad track ends and becomes a narrow path, descending to cross streams before reaching the rocky gorge containing Measand Beck (1). A concrete bridge takes you over the beck, followed by a short rise to cross the low end of Sandhill Knotts before running on across more open fellside rising steeply on the right to the vast moorland reaches of High Raise and Long Grain.

Near Pultsgill Sike the path is ushered between tumbledown walls that are a poignant reminder that this was once an inhabited landscape, sacrificed in the 1930s to quench the thirst of some distant conurbation.

Pleasant walking ensues on the approach to the great hollow of Whelter Bottom, traversing steep slopes, undulating in spectacular fashion. Finally, the path descends through bracken, beside which more collapsed stone walls leading down to the water's edge from the intake wall remind again that an isolated farming community once lived and worked in Mardale. A sturdy footbridge crosses Whelter Beck, cascading down a narrow ravine lined with holly bushes, rowan and alder. Above, the broken form of Whelter Crag rises steeply on the right, its grassy flanks invariably grazed by red deer.

Beyond the footbridge, the path courts the intake wall before moving away to cross the snout of Birks Crag and Castle Crag, the site of an ancient British hill fort. The ongoing path descends steeply as it approaches Riggindale, where it meanders through field enclosures, passing below a small wall-enclosed woodland. Rough Crag rises directly ahead and, as you round the edge of the woodland, the lower, craggy slopes of Kidsty Pike come into view. A sharp change of direction leads down to cross

View across Haweswater to High Raise

Randale Beck by a stone bridge, followed by a brief interlude of grassy terrain before a wooden footbridge across Riggindale Beck.

The path is then channelled between two rows of low upright stone to reach a compact flight of stone steps and more upright stones leading to and through a small stand of larch. The way ahead now lies to the right of the prominent, wooded end of Rough Crag, known as The Rigg. Across this ridge, the path descends gently to find its way around the head of the lake, by footbridges and gates, to reach the car park at the road head (2).

At the northern edge of the car park go through a small gap in a low wall on to the lakeshore path. Throughout its length the path never strays far from the road wall, often pressing close up beside it, a visually limiting factor of no importance since all the views, and stunning they are, lie across the reservoir into Riggindale, Whelter Bottom and Fordingdale. For much of its course, the path undulates, dipping and div-ing through old enclosures to reach a narrow stone footbridge spanning Hopgill Beck.

Cross the bridge, and at a wall gap, follow the path ahead (signposted: Burnbanks). The path climbs out of the gill and then contours across slopes of bracken, hawthorn and holly. As the path approaches a reservoir control tower it suddenly confronts a small woodland. Climb up

Start/Finish Burnbanks, GR 508161. Limited parking opposite telephone box – please do not obstruct garages

Distance 17km (10½ miles)

Height gain Many undulations, probably totalling about 300m (985ft)

Walking time 4½–5 hours

Type of walk Entirely low level, on good paths throughout most of the route. Splendid scenery, and a fine all-season walk

The Route in Brief

Start Leave Burnbanks village on a broad track rounding the edge of woodland to reach the open fell at a gate. Continue along a broad trail to Measand Beck.

1 Cross beck and continue to reach Whelter Bottom and then Riggindale, before reaching the head of the lake (car park).

2 Go through gap in low wall to follow signposted path, never far from wall, to reach the road near the dam.

3 Follow road to Naddle Bridge and turn L into oak woodland to return to Burnbanks.

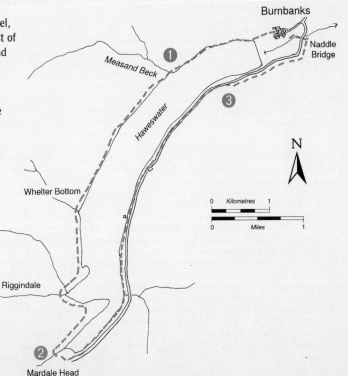

to the right here, to find a gloomy path sandwiched tightly between the wall and the trees. This ends at a flight of steps leading down to the tower. Cross the steps, to continue below the wall, shortly descending to meet an access track below a gate.

The path continues to run below the wall but for a short distance is less evident. If necessary, join the valley road and walk down it for a short distance to the next gate, where you can rejoin the shore path to a footbridge and wall gap.

Now you engage some delightful prime woodland, and encounter a number of places where the path crosses narrow ledges above steep drops to the reservoir. Frequently, as if afraid to leave its protection, the path clings to the wall, and as a result you pass by the Haweswater Hotel completely unaware of its existence. Elsewhere, the path meanders through the lowest edges of Guerness Wood, where raised tree roots can trip the unwary or the weary.

With the dam in sight, the path weaves behind an old boathouse, before finally rising to the road at a gate **(3)**, beside which a commemorative plaque announces the route's dedication to Bill Foster.

On the road, go left, and follow it round as far as Naddle Bridge. Cross the bridge and turn left into oak woodland, a sylvan glade that for Coast-to-Coast walkers effectively marks the end of Lakeland and the start of the limestone fringe *en route* for Kirkby Stephen. Past the woodland go through a wall gap, and left along the road back to the starting point.

LOADPOT HILL TO HIGH RAISE

Sandwiched between the long valleys of Martindale and Mardale, the grassy pudding-shaped fells that roll northwards from High Raise probably receive far fewer walkers than any other group of Lakeland fells. On a fine day, long distance walkers on the Northern Coast to Coast Walk may cross them as an alternative to a low-level passage along the western shore of Haweswater. Otherwise, their only visitors will be ardent peak-baggers, solitude-seekers and the idly curious.

The whole range is traversed by the Roman road, High Street. That alone commends interest, but if you enjoy moorland wandering, and can cope with the inevitable diversions to avoid sporadic peat hags and boggy depressions, then the Loadpot Hill-High Raise ridge deserves your attention.

The walk starts in the village of Burnbanks, built in 1929 to house construction workers building the Haweswater Reservoir and dam. Burnbanks is a sad sight now, with many of the houses demolished or derelict and an air of fateful resignation settled upon it like a patina of neglect.

As you enter the village a surfaced track starts off on the right and this is the way to go. You can reach it from a small parking area in front of garages, by walking up a narrow path beside the telephone box.

Follow the track out of the village, to reach the edge of woodland, where it bends right and left to a gate in a boundary fence. A good track continues beside the plantation and accompanies either a wall or fence (on the left) across the base of low brackeny hillocks. Across the reservoir the wooded slopes of Naddle Forest rise to a minor top, Hugh's Laithes Pike, which is said to mark the last resting place of a local ne'er-do-good, Jimmie Lowther, who broke his neck steeplechasing while drunk – an early case of drunken driving!

You need only follow the broad track to the narrow rocky gorge of Measand Beck (1). By then the track has narrowed to a path leading to a bridge over the beck. Here, and up above, Measand Beck produces a splendid display of ravine cascades, known as The Forces, and in pre-reservoir days developed an enormous fan of gravel and boulders that almost reached the far side of the valley.

Having crossed Measand Beck, leave the main path and turn immediately right, climbing through bracken to follow the line of the

beck to another bridge re-crossing the beck. Here you are at the entrance to the hanging valley of Fordingdale, one of Lakeland's almost forgotten dales, but well worth exploring.

From the second bridge the way is less clear. Continue not up the valley but along the line of a tributary of Measand Beck (west of north) to a low col, east of Low Kop (2), where the remains of an old quarry (GR 479164) and a building tell of more toilsome times before the advent of mechanical diggers. From the quarry a good track leads westwards above the rim of Fordingdale to the southern-most of Wether Hill's two summits. On the way, you can cut across to the northern mound, which is the higher, its top marked by a large cairn, though there is slightly higher ground to the east.

To the north rises Loadpot Hill. You can reach it more directly from Burnbanks via the lonely valley of Cawdale, but inflowing tributaries and associated boggy going makes this an unappetising prospect. Wether Hill and Loadpot Hill, however, are linked by a good path passing a mound of rubble, all that remains of Lowther House, a shooters' lodge. It is known that in days gone by Lady Lonsdale was accustomed to drive in her carriage to Lowther House for lunch.

Along the Haweswater Shore Path

Loadpot Hill carries a trig pillar with a small cairn and boundary stone a short distance away. From it you retrace your steps to Wether Hill, to begin the long, gently undulating stroll to High Raise, accompanied, at various distances, by a wire fence and a wall. You traverse a few minor bumps, Red Crag and Raven Howe, before finally easing upwards to High Raise (3), on which a spread of rocks and stones has been gathered into a large cairn-shelter. In spite of enjoying a commanding position above Ramps Gill, with fine views to the west, the High Raise shelter prefers to turn its attention eastwards, to the high summits of the Pennines.

From High Raise continue following the Roman road on to the stony edge of Rampsgill Head (which of course you can visit for good measure), before heading southeast to Kidsty Pike, from where a long, easy descent eastwards leads to Kidsty Howes. Here the path steepens and changes direction as it drops to Riggindale Beck (4). As you approach the valley bottom you can bear left to a stone bridge spanning Randale Beck. A brief climb takes you to the edge of a plantation. With this on your left, wander through derelict field enclosures before engaging the delightful, undulating traverse to the wide hollow of Whelter Bottom. From here you simply follow the Northern Coast to Coast route, a good, clear path, all the way back to Measand Beck and Burnbanks.

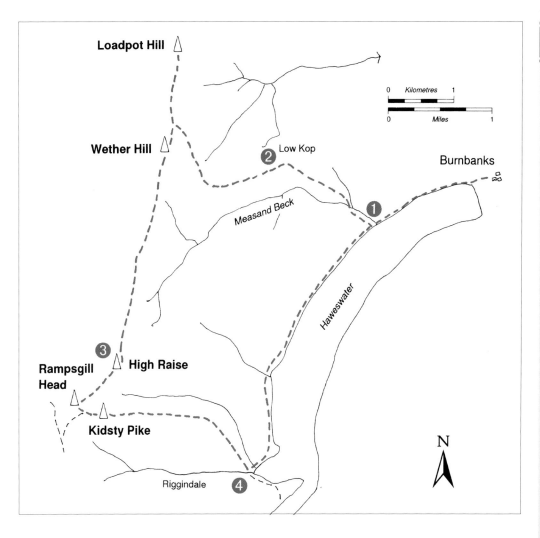

Loadpot Hill

Wether Hill

Low Kop
②

Burnbanks

Measand Beck

①

Haweswater

③ High Raise

Rampsgill Head

Kidsty Pike

Riggindale ④

0   Kilometres   1

0   Miles   1

N

FACT FILE

Start/Finish Burnbanks, GR 508161. Limited parking opposite telephone box — please do not obstruct garages
Distance 21.5km (13$\frac{1}{2}$ miles)
Height gain 800m (2625ft)
Walking time 7 hours
Type of walk Generally easy walking over peaty moorland heights, finishing along a good path along the west shore of Haweswater. Can be confusing in mist in places

The Route in Brief

Start From Burnbanks village take the higher of two lanes, leading out of the village to reach a boundary gate at the edge of woodland. Continue along the track that follows as far as Measand Beck.
1 Cross the beck and turn immediately R, following the beck upstream to a higher bridge. Cross the bridge and follow a tributary to Low Kop.
2 Follow path running W to Wether Hill. Visit Loadpot Hill (N) and return, continuing S along Roman road to High Raise.
3 Go round to Kidsty Pike and descend E and SE to reach Riggindale.
4 Cross Randale Beck and follow undulating path above west shoreline of Haweswater back to Burnbanks.

AROUND RIGGINDALE

It looks so simple on the map, that arrow-straight dashed green line running east-west along Rough Crag on the south side of Riggindale. Try to follow it and you will experience a few surprises, and more than likely incur the wrath of the Royal Society for the Protection of Birds. Closer scrutiny of the map reveals a more sensible line a little to the south, one that underfoot becomes an outstanding ridge walk with none of the intricacies that might deter walkers on Striding Edge or Sharp Edge. Once the ridge is ascended, the walk visits High Street before circling around the head of Riggindale for a return via Kidsty Pike, probably the most prominent of the eastern fells when seen from the M6 motorway, to the east.

The walk begins from the car park at the road end in Mardale. Parking is limited so arrive early. Go through the nearby gate and turn right beside a wall, to cross Mardale Beck, and right again, heading for the mature stand of larch and spruce that colonise The Rigg (1). As you approach the trees, the path starts rising and finally meets the low end of a ridge at a gap in a wall.

Go left, over a small hillock, with the formidable end of Rough Crag towering above you. It seems impregnable, but a path threads a way through or round all obstacles on the way, leaving you free to concentrate on heart and lungs. The going is far less rough than the name suggests but it remains steep, at least until the summit (marked by a large cairn) is reached.

The view from the ridge never fails to impress. To the south lies a deep bowl containing Blea Water, overlooked by the slopes of High Street; to the north, Kidsty Pike, the final top of the day, rises above the wide cove of Riggindale. Golden eagles are often seen above Riggindale and the surrounding fells, though their eyrie is zealously guarded by members of the Royal Society for the Protection of Birds. You can ease their vigil by keeping strictly to the path over Rough Crag during the breeding season (from mid-March to September).

Continue along the ridge and descend a little to a grassy col, Caspel Gate, where there is a small pond. Beyond this you engage an airy,

Left: Across Haweswater to Rough Crag
Right: Looking down on Riggindale

Start/Finish Mardale Head car park,
GR 469107
Distance 12km (7½ miles)
Height gain 675m (2215ft)
Walking time 4½–5 hours
Type of walk Rough and steep to begin,
followed by mainly grassy slopes

The Route in Brief

Start Leave the car park at Mardale Head and
walk round the lake to The Rigg.

1 Turn L and ascend Rough Crag, crossing its top
and continuing up Long Stile to High Street.
2 Go N along wall and cross the Straits of
Riggindale, following path round to Kidsty Pike.
3 Descend long grassy slopes (E), then SE to
reach bridge across Riggindale Beck.
4 Follow path to The Rigg and retrace steps.

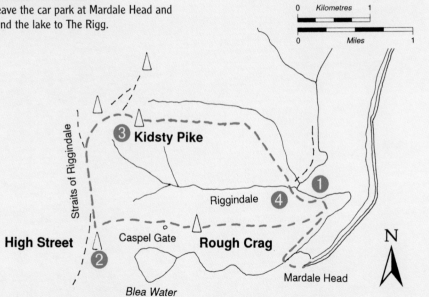

twisting path ascending Long Stile, finally reaching the northern end of High Street **(2)**. The summit lies a couple of minutes south and the simplest way of finding it in mist is to walk ahead (west) from the top of Long Stile until you intersect a dilapidated wall, and then follow this left (south) to the trig pillar.

Return north beside the wall to the Straits of Riggindale where wall and the course of the Roman road for which High Street is renowned, squeeze across a narrow neck of land high above Riggindale. When the path forks, you should branch right across the top of Twopenny Crag, heading directly for Kidsty Pike. A brief diversion northwards from this path will bring you on to Rampsgill Head from where there is a fine view into the depths of Martindale.

To complete the short stretch on to Kidsty Pike's rocky topknot simply go back to the path and follow it round. On a clear day you can make a beeline for it. From this eyrie-like vantage point **(3)** you gaze out across the deep hollow of Riggindale, as eagles might.

Straightforward grassy slopes now send you racing down towards Mardale Head, until the craggy rise of Kidsty Howes deflects you south-east. Steep slopes lead down to the footbridge **(4)** over Riggindale Beck beyond which a clear path runs on to regain The Rigg, from where you can retrace your steps to the car park.

THE THREE PASSES WALK

I t was while working on another book during the 1980s that I first realised the possibility of linking three passes in the eastern fells to make an acceptable day's circuit. No doubt many walkers had already had the same idea, so I claim no originality, indeed all the passes – Gatescarth, Nan Bield and Kentmere-Longsleddale – have been in use by packhorses and trans-valley merchants for hundreds of years, though only a keen walker's mentality would think of making a complete circuit. This round is an excellent way of getting to know these far eastern fells of Lakeland, and though the walk can be done in all seasons, care and proper equipment (including an ice axe) are vital in winter when the Nan Bield Pass in particular can pose difficulties.

The logical place to start is Mardale road head car park, because it allows you to tackle the highest and toughest pass first. Sadgill works almost as well but has limited parking, while a start from Kentmere involves some cross-field walking to reach the

Nan Bield Pass

start of the pass into Longsleddale. Nor does it much matter which way round you go, though anti-clockwise is here preferred.

From the car park go through the nearby gate and take the left branch of the path ahead to a signpost for Kentmere. Initially poor, the path almost immediately improves, and though the going is rough, the scenery more than compensates and the tumbling becks, Small Water Beck in particular, provide delightful accompaniment to your labours. As you ascend a view opens up of the wide corrie below High Street in which Blea Water reposes, but the way lies past another tarn, Small Water, which is a useful excuse for a breather. Beyond, the path clambers energetically to the shelter standing on the narrow col that is the Nan Bield Pass (1). If you turn round you will be rewarded with a stunning view stretching as far as Cross Fell and the high Pennines. To the south, the cone of Ill Bell rises darkly above Kentmere Reservoir, which in the scorching summer of 1995 was dry.

A series of zigzags leads you down the other side of Nan Bield, with the gradient easing all the time. Pleasant walking down the valley ensues, keeping high on the fellside until you are opposite the reservoir and below Smallthwaite Knott from where a gradual descent takes you to river level and the continuing path to Overend Farm. Go through

Haweswater from Nan Bield Pass

the left of two gates and along a surfaced road until, just beyond a sheepfold (bridleway signpost nearby) you can move right on a grassy track, through a gate, and back on to a surfaced lane rising to the left. At a signpost for a bridleway to Mardale, go through a gate and follow a lane for a short distance to another lane on the left, signposted to Longsleddale. This now leads you up and over the second pass of the day and runs on down to reach the valley at Sadgill Bridge (2).

From the bridge, go left and follow the walled quarry lane heading up the valley below the cliffs of Buckbarrow Crag. This is easy, delightful walking, in the company of the River Sprint, which boasts a number of fine cascades and seems to go on for ever. As you approach the head of the valley the track moves left to the area of Wrengill Quarry, one of the oldest, if not *the* oldest quarry in the Lakes. Follow this quarry road until it ends, beyond a gate, from where a narrow path moves away from the wall to ascend the Gatescarth Pass which often tends to be wet near its summit (3). On your right the slopes rise to Branstree, and on the left to Adam Seat, both worthwhile summits but often neglected.

Over the pass a splendid descent follows, back to the head of Mardale, once more confronting you with steep, craggy fellsides to admire, along with a fine prospect of Haweswater. The descending path brings you back to the car park.

FACT FILE

Start/Finish Mardale Head car park, GR 469107
Distance 16km (10 miles)
Height gain 870m (2855ft)
Walking time 5–6 hours
Type of walk On good paths through splendid scenery. Nowhere difficult, but long and tiring

The Route in Brief

Start Begin from the Mardale Head car park, through a gate and follow the path, signposted to Kentmere, that rises past Small Water to Nan Bield Pass.
1 Descend in zigzags into the Kent valley and continue to Overend Farm, pressing on to reach a lane, running L (signposted to Longsleddale). Cross the pass and descend to Sadgill.
2 At Sadgill Bridge, go L along walled lane to reach the vicinity of Wrengill Quarries, and ascend Gatescarth Pass.
3 Descend back to Mardale.

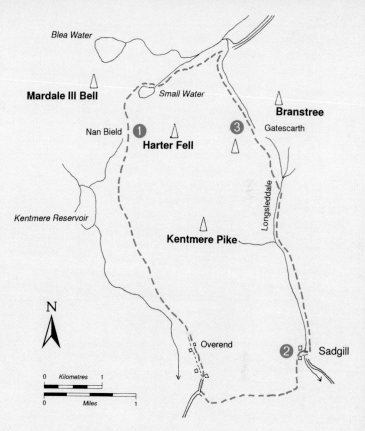

GREY CRAG AND TARN

Longsleddale, formed by the River Sprint, is one of the most attractive of the eastern dales of Lakeland and graphically displays a clear transition from rocks of the Borrowdale Volcanic Series, north of Sadgill, to the softer Silurian deposits to the south. To the west rises the long ridge over Shipman Knotts and Kentmere Pike, while to the east Sleddale Fell poses more than a few problems of route-finding in poor visibility.

This visit to two of the components of Sleddale Fell, known intimately as Grey Crag and Tarn Crag, crosses some rough and trackless terrain before descending to the head of the valley for a leisurely stroll back to the start.

Longsleddale is a working valley, so to minimise obstruction the walk begins from the hamlet of Stockdale, where you will find an outdoor pursuits centre, a café and a sizeable parking area.

Go north-east up the lane past the buildings to a gate and continue to near the confluence of Stockdale Beck and Brow Gill where you will find two gates. Go through the left gate, and then right, beside Stockdale Beck ascending to a gate in a wall. Between you and Grey Crag (1) now lies trackless, grassy terrain punctuated with rock outcrops and crossed by fences and collapsed walls, none of which bar progress to the lonely summit.

There is a surprisingly good view from Grey Crag, especially to the east and southwards, embracing the lesser known Borrowdale, the puddings of the Howgills, and the Pennine summits south of Kirkby Stephen, flanking the Vale of Eden. On Tarn Crag is a pillar constructed during the building of the Haweswater Reservoir in the early 1930s, and this will prove to be a helpful target.

On a clear day, crossing to Tarn Crag (2) involves little more than moorland wandering, doing your best to evade the occasional clutches of bog and the remnants of Greycrag Tarn, which I have yet to find with water in it, though there is plenty sponged into the ground around it. On a day less than clear, you shouldn't be here.

You can extend the day a little by walking out to the fine cairn that stands on Harrop

Sadgill, Longsleddale

FACT FILE

Start/Finish Stockdale, GR 491054
Distance 9km (5½ miles)
Height gain 540m (1770ft)
Walking time 3–4 hours
Type of walk Mainly trackless moorland and not advised other than on a clear day

The Route in Brief

Start Leave Stockdale by a lane heading NE and climb through gates and beside Stockdale Gill to reach the open fell and a straightforward pull to the summit of Grey Crag.
1 Head NW to pass Greycrag Tarn (or branch R to Harrop Pike first), and ascend to the pillar on Tarn Crag.
2 Continue N to meet a fence and follow this down to a col at the head of Mosedale.
3 Turn L to descend to the head of Longsleddale, and L again, on a broad trail, between walls, heading down the valley to Sadgill and Stockdale.

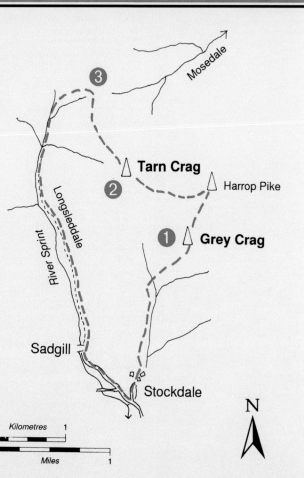

Pike, before trekking back to Tarn Crag. If you then head north from Tarn Crag you meet a fence, with a faint path beside it that guides you safely down to a gate on the wild col (**3**) between Longsleddale and Mosedale. Go left here to drop to the head of Longsleddale at Brownhowe Bottom. Just across the head of the dale, the disused Wrengill Quarry is probably the oldest of the Lakeland quarries, being mentioned in a document written during the reign of Edward I (1272–1307).

When you reach the head of the dale, go left and follow the long, walled track back to Sadgill and Stockdale, with the growing River Sprint proving a delightful companion as you press on below a surprising array of crags, notably Buckbarrow Crag. The walking is easy after the tussocky trials of the tops and makes a leisurely stroll on a fine spring day.

THE KENTMERE HORSESHOE

Performing a long, extended loop around Kentmere Common and the Kent valley, this walk is a firm favourite with walkers of all ages. Winter conditions pose a problem or two on some of the descents, but otherwise the circuit is a splendid outing and deserves everyone's attention – but not all at the same time!

Opinions differ about which way round is best. Most seem to go clockwise, as here. This gets four summits rattled off quickly, each involving ascent and descent that can be tiring towards the end of a day, leaving the relatively easier walking for the second half. It also has the advantage that if you are feeling weary by the time you reach Nan Bield Pass you can escape back to Kentmere at least having done six summits. An anti-clockwise circuit on the other hand is likely to provide fewer walking companions.

Kentmere has very limited parking, so get there early. From July to October there is a weekend only bus service into Kentmere from Staveley, which will ease congestion in this narrow valley. For information ring Stagecoach Cumberland on 01946 63222.

From St Cuthbert's Church, follow the road as it sets off for the Garburn Pass. The route is well signposted, and, as the metalled road comes to an end, go right on a signposted path. The track is then stony, but rises gently above the valley, with attractive glimpses of low fells, farms and cottages. Craggy outcrops dot the lower slopes of Yoke, on your right; indeed the area is known as the Crag Quarter.

At a bend, a tempting path heads upwards to a broad gully, near Buck Crag. I once left a young couple to plod up that way, while I followed the continuing path to the top of Garburn Pass. I reached the top twenty minutes ahead of the couple; evidently the Buck Crag short cut is a more leisurely approach. At the top of the pass turn right through a gate (1) to follow a grassy trod, never far from a long wall. When the wall changes direction, cross it and climb on to the broad end of Yoke, from where a clear path runs up to the summit (2).

I once described the early part of this walk as far as Yoke, as having 'a certain dreariness, but not sufficient to detract from the overall sensation of a fine excursion'. Years on, I recognise the dreariness as youthful impatience to be on the tops; now I savour the homely beauty of the valleys as I head for the heights. And what heights! From Yoke the view is of mountains stacked on mountains, seeming to flow endlessly away in all directions.

The next summit along the ridge is Ill Bell, a shapely cone recognisable from afar, and topped by a rough and craggy summit littered with cairns. A clear path above Star Crag and Rainsborrow Cove links Yoke and Ill Bell and continues across the top of a steep drop into Over Cove and Kentmere Reservoir, to Froswick, a miniature replica of Ill Bell.

Thornthwaite Crag (3) now awaits, pinned to the landscape by an enormous cairn. The long approach seems daunting but easily succumbs to a steady plod. Again the excellent path continues its duty, branching left as it meets the line of the Roman road crossing the top of Gavel Crag, bound for High Street and beyond. Stroll on steadily and you will find the wall and low rock outcrops that mark the top of Thornthwaite Crag to be a perfect place for a break, possessing a fine view west over Stony Cove Pike and Red Screes, and south into the valley of Trout Beck.

A good path setting off south of east and curving north-east takes you round to High

Street on the line of the Roman road. The road, however, does not cross the summit of High Street, so leave it as you approach a wall, and accompany the wall to the trig pillar.

Return beside the wall to continue on a clear path that crosses a grassy link to Mardale Ill Bell. On a clear day you can head straight for Mardale Ill Bell from High Street. This last of the Kentmere west side fells forms a thumb of land separating Kentdale and Mardale, and by moving north for a short distance from the main path as you reach the cairned summit, you discover a stunning view of Blea Water nestling in its corrie below.

Continue with the path across Mardale Ill Bell and follow its descent to Nan Bield Pass (4), an ancient packhorse route. 'Nant' derives from the Welsh and means a brook or a gorge, while 'bield' means a sheltered place. A small shelter sits in the middle of the narrow col.

If you have had enough at this stage, turn right, down the pass and along a clear route back to Kentmere, picking up the rest of this route description as it comes down from Shipman Knotts to meet the walled High Lane. Otherwise, engage first gear and begin the grind up on to Harter Fell. To be truthful, the pull is nothing like as difficult or as long as it seems, rising in two easy stages to a

Ill Bell summit

large cairn not far from a fence and small boundary stone.

The fence, and later a wall, is now your guide to Kentmere Pike, speeding across springy, but sometimes boggy turf to reach the few rocks that cap the disappointing summit; even the trig pillar hides from sight on the other side of the wall.

A short way on, the wall becomes a fence again and the path divides, sending a long track racing down to a stile over a wall. If you want a speedy return to the valley, this is the way to go. It meets the path from Nan Bield Pass near Hallow Bank.

For Shipman Knotts, ignore this diversion and follow the fence to Goat Scar and then on to a wall that crosses the top of Shipman Knotts (5). Beyond this rugged outlier, the wall leads you down to the top of the pass linking Kentdale and Longsleddale. Turn right here and follow a walled track down to Stile End, beyond which you soon connect with the Nan Bield route.

Now walk left along a walled lane (High Lane) (6) until, at a signposted through-stile, you can cross the wall and descend a field to Low Lane. Another stile accesses Low Lane and directly ahead you can cross another field to a footbridge over the Kent. Turn left to follow an obvious path back to the church in Kentmere. If you miss the through-stile on High Lane, simply follow the lane down until you can turn sharply right, descending a narrow lane down to Low Bridge.

FACT FILE

Start/Finish St Cuthbert's Church, Kentmere (very limited parking), GR 456041
Distance 20.5km (12³/₄ miles)
Height gain 1155m (3790ft)
Walking time 7 hours
Type of walk Long and with considerable height gain. Generally on good paths throughout

The Route in Brief

Start Walk along the road away from the church in Kentmere and take the signposted route to the top of Garburn Pass.

1 Through a gate turn R to follow a wall, crossed when it changes direction, to a path rising on to Yoke.

2 Continue on a clear path over Ill Bell and Froswick to Thornthwaite Crag.

3 Follow broad path round to High Street and then retreat to Mardale Ill Bell, and descend to Nan Bield Pass.

4 Ascend Harter Fell and follow fence/wall over Kentmere Pike to Shipman Knotts.

5 Descend to walled lane leading R to High Lane.

6 Turn L along High Lane to through-stile and descend two fields to cross River Kent. Go L on track back to church.

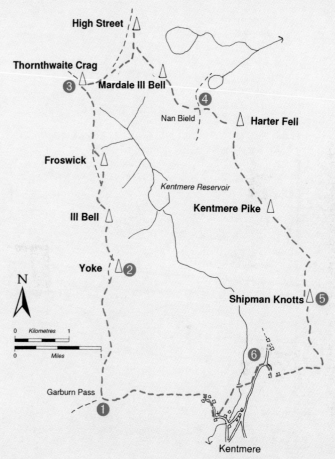

ACKNOWLEDGEMENTS & INDEX

I am particularly grateful to Dave Brown of DB Mountain Sports, Kendal, for the supply of boots, clothing and equipment, which kept me warm, dry and comfortable throughout the preparation of this book.

In addition, I much appreciate the generosity of Lakelovers of Bowness-on-Windermere for allowing me to use one of their excellent self-catering holiday homes.

Steve Yeates of the Ordnance Survey Press Office has very kindly supplied me with up-to-date Outdoor Leisure Maps, from which I have been able to deduce much reliable and vital information.